New Perspectives on Chinese Politics and Society

Series Editor
Yang Zhong
Shanghai Jiao Tong University
Shanghai, China

Rapid growth has posed new challenges for sustainable political and economic development in China. This series is dedicated to the study of modern Chinese politics and society, drawing on case studies, field work, surveys, and quantitative analysis. In addition to its empirical focus, this series will endeavour to provide unique perspectives and insights by publishing research from scholars based in China and the region. Forthcoming titles in this series will cover political culture, civil society, political economy and governance.

More information about this series at
http://www.palgrave.com/gp/series/14734

Chao Chen

Toleration

Group Governance in a Chinese Third Line Enterprise

Chao Chen
Xiamen University
Xiamen, Fujian, China

New Perspectives on Chinese Politics and Society
ISBN 978-981-10-8940-4   ISBN 978-981-10-8941-1   (eBook)
https://doi.org/10.1007/978-981-10-8941-1

Library of Congress Control Number: 2018940364

Cover Illustration: © xylo Alan King / Alamy Stock Photo

Printed on acid-free paper

This Palgrave Macmillan imprint is published by the registered company Springer Nature Singapore Pte Ltd. part of Springer Nature.
The registered company address is: 152 Beach Road, #21-01/04 Gateway East, Singapore 189721, Singapore

To all Chinese Third Line workers

ACKNOWLEDGMENTS

This book would not have been possible without the guidance of my adviser Dr. Erik Mobrand. Dr. Mobrand never strictly steered me in any particular direction. It is his open mind that enabled me to carry out an ethnographical research that explores an understudied community.

I am much indebted to my committee members, Professor Zheng Yongnian, Dr. Wang Cheng-Lung, and Professor Xu Youwei, an external member from Shanghai University. They have provided me with great support and invaluable suggestions.

I would like to thank the faculty and staff of the Department of Political Science of the National University of Singapore. Special thanks are due to Professor Jamie Davison, Professor Chen An, Professor Kim Sooyeon, Professor Janice Bially Mattern, Professor Luke O'Sullivan, and Dr. Kilkon Ko, who taught me a lot during my life in Singapore. I also owe a debt of gratitude to Ms. Noor Sham binte Abdul Hamid and Ms. Angeline Koh, who have always been very patient and helpful in explaining various policies of the university to me.

Moreover, I am very fortunate to have a group of friends from different departments at National University of Singapore (NUS). Special thanks are due to Li Xiang for his editing of this work and Wang Tong, Zhu Ruolei, Yueng Wing Yan, Liberty Chee, and Sabastiano Rwengabo for their constructive comments. In addition, I would also like to thank my dear roommates, Jin Xin, Yang Jing, Liu Xiao, Wang Guanfeng, Bian Jingwen, Shen Yanyan, Yang Jie, and Chai Bo. Living with them has made my life in a foreign country much more enjoyable.

Last but not least, I owe a gargantuan thank you to Mr. Ni Tongzheng and all his former colleagues at Jinjiang Factory, a group of long-suffering Third Line workers who made tremendous sacrifices and devoted their youths to the country's industrial development. Today, the same group of sexagenarians is offering as much as they can to a young man who they have never met before. This book is dedicated to them.

CONTENTS

LIST OF FIGURES

LIST OF TABLES

CHAPTER 1

Introduction

Located 50 miles northwest of Chengdu, the economic and trading center of southwestern China, is Danjingshan—a small town surrounded by stretches of rolling mountains. This mountainous terrain not only impeded the town's economic development but also isolated it from the outside world. However, at this hidden and primitive spot, a group of workers from many more developed cities on the east coast labored in a modern factory. This is the Jinjiang Oil Pump and Nozzle Factory (hereafter referred to as "Jinjiang Factory"), the field site of this study.

In fact, Jinjiang Factory is not the only example of this strange template. Similar factories and workers can be found in the remote areas of almost all the southwestern and northwestern provinces of China (see Fig. 1.1). These factories are called "Third Line Enterprises" and the workers are called "Third Line Workers". They are products of an immense but secret industrial project that began in the 1960s and ended in the 1980s. In the context of China's history, it is called the Third Line Construction[1] (Li and Jiang 2005; Meng 2013).

In the 1960s, China's security was facing two potential threats. Internationally, China was not on good terms with either of the two superpowers. Domestically, the country's industrial capacity and population were overwhelmingly concentrated in the east coast area. In order to maintain its industrial production in the event of war, the central government believed that it was essential to establish an alternative industrial base in western China. Out of this concern for security, from the early 1960s to the late 1970s, numerous factories and workers were transferred from

© The Author(s) 2018
C. Chen, *Toleration*, New Perspectives on Chinese Politics and
Society, https://doi.org/10.1007/978-981-10-8941-1_1

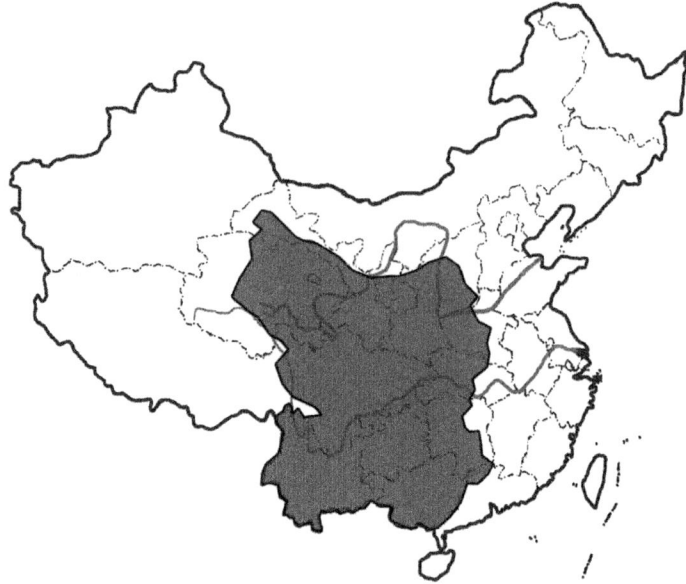

Fig. 1.1 The area of the Third Line Construction

cities on the east coast and the old northeast industrial base, such as Shanghai, Tianjin, Beijing, and Shenyang, to the desolate interior. By the early 1980s, in the area of the Third Line Construction, more than 1100 industrial projects had been completed (Yuan 2003; Meng 2013), about 29,000 enterprises established (Lin and Ji 1987), and nearly four million workers were transferred (Liu 2012).The industries were mostly related to the military. Mao stipulated that the construction of Third Line factories should follow the principle of "by the side of mountains, dispersion and being caved" (*kaoshan, fensan, jindong*). Hence, these factories and workers were covertly scattered in remote villages or mountain areas, isolated from the outside world. The Jinjiang Factory is just one of these secretly transferred factories.

The Third Line factories and their workers have received scant treatment in the existing literature on Chinese labor politics. Compared to the numerous and matured studies on urban SOEs in Mao's era and after, studies on the Third Line Construction mainly focused on its scale, influence, and historical significance to Chinese industrial development, while few have paid attention to its workplace politics and sociology (Naughton 1988; Mel 1993; Chan et al. 1996; Chen 2004; Bachman 2001; Dong 2001; Li and Jiang 2005; Bramall 2009). The confidentiality of the Third Line Construction and its remote locations may have deterred researchers. Published information on Third Line Enterprises is scant and there are few archival sources. In addition, many of the factories closed in the 1990s. A recent development that helped the author to investigate this subject is a resurgence of interest among retired former workers in Third Line Enterprises. Former participants in the Third Line are now composing memoirs, forming online communities, and holding events related to their history. In these activities, the author discovered a pathway to investigate this understudied topic. Drawing on untapped primary sources, this book addresses the gap in our understanding of Third Line Enterprises. In particular, this book asks the following question: what sort of industrial relations could be found in the Third Line Enterprises?

One important lesson introduced by the existing literature on urban SOEs is that even in these work units informal social ties outside the unit could shape management practices (Lee 1999; Gallagher 2005; Cai 2006). Geographic isolation in the Third Line Enterprises made the situation different—there were no pre-existing social relationships among workers and the social context. Under such unique circumstances, did managers have a freer hand in enforcing discipline due to the factory's isolation? Through an in-depth analysis of a typical Third Line enterprise, the Jinjiang Factory, I will show that geographic isolation did not actually lead to a stricter and harsher management. In contrast, it encouraged the creation of densely interconnected social networks within the factory. These networks promoted workers' control over the production process. As a result, isolation encouraged group managers to adapt by tolerating rule-breaking behavior, such as absenteeism.

In the analysis of industrial relations, this study mainly focuses on the level of group leaders. In Chinese factories, group leaders or supervisors are grassroots managers, who directly interact with workers on a daily basis. This unique position in the organizational hierarchy requires them to constantly juggle frequently conflicting demands of their upper managers and their member workers. Ideally, and according to the policies, group leaders should respond to the needs of their workers as a homogeneous group; in practice, they had to develop techniques to respond to the workers as heterogeneous individuals. To cope with these controversies, they make personal decisions, establish routines, and invent tactics. All of these decisions and inventions eventually set the context and create informal policies for workers to follow. In short, group leaders are not merely passive policy implementers but active policy makers and re-makers. Therefore, without detailed knowledge of the actual managerial behavior of group leaders, we can hardly understand what is really happening in the production line.

Because of this book's specific focus on worker–leader relations in the factory, there is no attempt to offer a full history of the Third Line Enterprises from the 1960s to the 1990s. Instead, the study attempts to shed light on the Third Line workers' lives during a particular period from the mid-1970s to the 1980s. This period marks the peak of operation for many Third Line Enterprises. In response to the perceived rising US threat, the planning of the Third Line Construction had emerged as early as in the mid-1960s. However, this construction was not widely implemented until the 1969–1971 period, when the threat from the Soviet Union was seemingly more and more urgent. As a result, the vast majority of the Third Line Enterprises were established in the early 1970s. In the 1990s, as market-oriented enterprise reforms started, the Third Line Enterprises faced two different fates. Many of them went bankrupt and disappeared. Those that survived were relocated into nearby cities and gradually transformed into normal urban state-owned enterprises (SOEs). The reforms of the 1990s put an end to the Third Line Enterprises as a unique form of workplace. Therefore, the onset of reform in the 1990s provides a natural endpoint for this study.

Although the Third Line Enterprises lasted for only about 20 years, they had tremendous significance for Chinese industry development and urbanization. Taking this unique group of factories as the research subject, this book makes contributions in three aspects. First, based on several interviews and fieldwork in a Third Line enterprise, this study provides analysis of first-hand materials on the Third Line workers who have long been unknown to, or maybe forgotten by, society, officials, and scholars. Second, with these valuable materials, this study for the first time systematically documents the daily life and working relations in the once-confidential Third Line Enterprises. Third, by knowing the Third Line workers' lives, this study draws attention to the varieties of industrial relations in pre-reform China. In a word, as an immense industrial project related to millions of Chinese in Mao's era, studies on the Third Line Enterprises and their workers have been missing from the existing literature and the significance of this study is to fill this gap.

To sum up, this is a book on industrial relations in a Third Line enterprise with a special focus on the level of group leaders' management. It is grounded in observations and interviews with workers and managers of Jinjiang Factory in Sichuan Province. The rest of the chapter is organized as follows. In the first section, I review two modes of managerial control in SOEs from the mid-1970s to the 1980s argued by previous studies. The second section explains the emergence of the tolerating strategy in Jinjiang Factory. Taking the group leaders' management of workers' absences as an example, the third section shows how the tolerating strategy manifested itself in practice. The fourth section is a discussion of the methodology for the fieldwork.

1.1   Managerial Control in SOEs from the Mid-1970s to the 1980s

Over the period from the mid-1970s to the 1980s, two modes of control in Chinese SOEs have been identified. Neo-traditionalism is arguably the only method of labor control prior to 1978, while "disorganized despotism" took shape in the 1980s. Do these models apply to the Third Line factories? In this section, I will show that due to the unique social structure in a Third Line factory, these modes of control are not applicable to the Third Line Enterprises. In addition, these modes suffer from one reductive problem: the interest of grassroots managers is assumed to fully overlap with that of their upper managers. As a result, the contextual differences and the analytical limitation make the previous studies ineffective in understanding the workplace order of the Third Line Enterprises. It is worth noting that the point here is not to challenge or replace the conventional wisdom. Instead, it is to highlight the diversity of forms of management–labor relations in China until the early reform era.

Neo-traditionalism: Managerial Control Before 1978

In the analysis of Chinese industrial relations prior to 1978, the significance of the work unit system has attracted many scholars' attention. Through their observations in industrial, medical, and technical units (Blecher and White 1979; Henderson and Cohen 1984; Yang 1989), these scholars independently come to a similar conclusion that the work unit in China "is not merely a type of workplace, but a long-standing and multifaceted institution that has served many purposes for the regime" (Lü and Perry 1997).

By far, the most influential study on Chinese work unit politics, however, is Andrew Walder's seminal work *Communist Neo-traditionalism*. In this book, Walder provides a comprehensive analytical framework to study authority in Chinese industry and argues that authority relations in contemporary Chinese industry are neo-traditional (Walder 1986). Specifically, in Chinese enterprises, the workers are no longer dependent on the foremen but the enterprises and the party-state. Neo-traditionalism can therefore be seen as a new form of dependence present in modern economic organizations. This new pattern of industrial relations, as Walder argues, has two institutional features. The first is the "organized dependence" (Lu 1989; Li 1993; Lü and Perry 1997; Frazier 2002), which consists of three sub-features: (1) workers are assumed to be immobile and economically dependent on their enterprises; (2) they are politically monopolized by the party and managed by the factory; and (3) they are personally supervised by their immediate leaders with many conceivable needs and benefits (Walder 1986, p. 13). Therefore, employment in the communist state enterprises does not reflect a market relationship but rather the state's political control over the workers (p. 12). In these enterprises, the workers gain not only their livelihood but also sociopolitical services and even social identities.

This organized dependence sets up the institutional basis for the second feature of neo-traditionalism, the patron–client relationship in the workplace. This clientelist link is not widely established among workers, but between supervisors and a minority of workers labeled activists. With the help of these activist workers, the party is able to extend its control to the bottom of the social order and, in return, these workers would receive preferential treatment from the management, such as greater job mobility, material benefits, and higher social status (Walder 1986, p. 246–47). In practice, this patronage relationship rests on a very subjective and ambiguous evaluation of workers' individual display (*biaoxian*). In the process of this evaluation, the political thinking, work attitude, performance, and level of skill are the basic criteria used by workers to judge themselves and their co-workers. Based on these judgments, the group leader rates each worker's individual result and reports the scores to his senior managers. Eventually, these scores become the workers' evidence for rewards and punishments.

At the heart of the two features is the Chinese workers' intertwined personal and institutional dependencies: that is, the workers' public loyalties to the party are mixed with their personal loyalties to the leader-patron (p. 247). However, workers' dependence on group leaders does not mean that the latter can willfully act without considering their members. This compromising role is determined by their unique intermediate positions. According to Walder (p. 103), the group leaders are "political brokers in the fullest sense of the term". In the workplace, they are not only the "feet" of the senior managers, relaying messages from above for their recognition, but also the "head" of the workers, yielding enough to their members' wishes to gain their cooperation. Though the link between reward and work performance is indirect and flexible, Walder (p. 112) argues that, in order to gain workers' cooperation, group leaders must ensure that non-work criteria do not obscure the linkage between performance and reward and maintain the perception of fairness among members. This implies that, however differential the distribution of interests may be, perceived fairness in the group is necessary. However, in his later discussion, Walder (1986, p. 170) focuses exclusively on the differentiating effect of the patron–client relationship, but remains silent on how the perceived fairness could be maintained. Ironically, a perceived *unfairness* is fully evident in his informant's account:

> As an activist, you have to choose between supporting the party and the other workers. So there is no longer any trust or affection with the other workers…but the shop director would always support the activists and try to make them feel better. They call meetings to tell the workers to stop attacking and sabotaging the activists. (Informant no. 72)

This informant reveals the fact that workers are able not only to perceive the unfairness in the workplace but also to tell the initiator of this unfairness. This raises a practical problem with the patronage–authority relationship. If the unfairness and its initiator can be identified, how can the group leaders motivate other members who are non-activists? This problem is even more pressing when the power of workers is taken into account. As many critiques have shown, the crucial limitation of Walder's analysis is his ignorance of workers' strength (Womack 1991; Zhou 1999). In the communist state enterprises, permanent employment status has contradictory effects on the control of labor. On one hand, it firmly bonds the workers to their workplace; on the other, it provides them with influential bargaining power. Moreover, the workers can also employ their "weapons of the weak", for example, footdrag, sabotage, to resist the unwelcome policies (Womack 1991, p. 327). In a word, the leaders are not as strong, and the workers are not as weak, as they are stereotypically portrayed. If so, how do group leaders appease the workers' discontent? How will they deal with workers' uncooperative misbehavior? These questions remain unanswered.

In fact, compared to the urban SOEs, workers in the Third Line Enterprises have more resources to counteract the management's exercise of authority. The most influential of these is their densely interconnected social structure. Isolated from the outside, these industrial workers had to reconstruct their friendship circles and seek their marital partners among their colleagues. Overtime, workers become integrated by these intimate ties. Popular saying among workers such as "No news is news the next morning" and "One twig shakes and hundreds will follow" give a vivid description of the interconnectedness of relationships. Neo-traditionalism cannot therefore be applied to the Third Line Enterprises, due to not only its theoretical limitations but also the contextual differences.

Disorganized Despotism: Managerial Control from 1978 to the 1980s

In the 1980s, the Chinese government initiated a series of industrial reforms aiming to improve the factory's performance. According to Lee Ching Kwan (1999), these reforms have, like opening Pandora's box, unleashed institutional and social forces that produce different factory regimes co-existing under the permissive banner of "market socialism". Specifically, she argues that these reforms have eroded the institutional foundations for neo-traditionalism in the pre-reform days. As a result, organized dependence—the crucial institutional feature of neo-traditionalism—is replaced by the labor regime she calls "disorganized despotism".

According to Lee, "disorganized" refers to a context in which the previously coherently organized state socialism begins to fall apart due to uncoordinated reform measures. In this context, the despotic regime takes shape and it bears three aspects of labor-management relations: labor's institutional dependence on production work for a livelihood, the imposition of coercive methods of labor control, and workers' collective apprehension of such control as being violations of their material interests and moral precepts (Lee 1999, p. 46). Under the regime of "disorganized despotism", day-to-day productions on the shop floor are filled with an overtly coercive method of labor control, the infliction of economic penalties, the proliferation of conflicts, and the demise of patron–clientelism (Lee 1999).

Lee's argument is supported by Zhao and Nichols' work. Based on 120 interviews at three state cotton mills, Zhao and Nichols (1996) conclude that China's industrial reforms in the 1980s and early 1990s have altered the relationship between party, trade union, workers, and managers at the enterprise level. In such a situation, workers are increasingly exploited by managers through a number of draconian practices such as longer working hours, increased quotas, and employing the full-load work method (Zhao and Nichols 1996). In the words of the authors, some of these practices "bring to mind management techniques employed during the stage of capitalist primitive accumulation" (p. 20).

Based on observations in different SOEs, however, other scholars argue differently, and some of them even come to an opposite conclusion. Blecher (1997) presents a path-dependent pattern of Chinese industrial relations in the 1980s. According to him, despite almost a decade of reforms, the pre-existing work unit system has not yet been fundamentally overturned. In many longer-established SOEs, managers continue to be affected by traditions formed during the Maoist period. They are not structurally induced to promote efficiency, productivity, and profits; they sustain a genuine commitment to the welfare of the working class and avoid outbursts of radical worker militancy. As a result, workers continue to enjoy some de facto job security and social welfare benefits such as housing and health care. In a word, the industrial reforms of the 1980s have hardly penetrated the labor process in China's SOEs (Zhao and Nichols 1996).

In stark contrast to the "disorganized despotism" argued by Lee, Walder (1987), in his later work, points out that the unchanged situation in state enterprises, especially the good job security and a weak link between performance and compensation, even strengthens the workers' bargaining power and influences the distributions of benefits in an egalitarian way. Gallagher (2005) adds that the development of a domestic private sector with foreign investment provides workers, especially new entrants into the workforce, with more opportunities outside the state sectors. The expansion of non-state sectors in the reform period therefore further increases workers' bargaining power over their managers.

Despite her denial of the existence of "disorganized despotism" in SOEs, Gallagher (2005) acknowledges that despotic management does exist in foreign-invested firms. Dorothy Solinger (1997) similarly points to an important difference in managerial control between SOEs and private foreign-invested firms. She argues that, in terms of worker welfare, state-owned firms continue to offer their workers major benefits, while foreign-owned enterprises represent a "throwback to the totally unregulated laissez-faire capitalism of the mid-nineteenth century".

As shown above, the authors mentioned earlier find salient differences caused at least in part by the problem of case-selection bias. For example, Lee's argument on "disorganized despotism" is based on her observations mainly in labor-intensive, non-strategic, and non-state-monopoly sectors such as camera factories, textile mills, and dyeing firms. The confirming evidence in Zhao and Nichols' work is from a similar industry (three state cotton mills). In the large, strategic, capital-intensive, and state monopoly sectors, however, the work unit system remains and disorganized despotism has not developed (Naughton 1997). The different influences of the reform on a factory's managerial control reveal a fact that the labor regime of the 1980s is diversified and closely related to the firm's ownership and the industrial type to which it belongs. In terms of these two factors, the Third Line Enterprises are typical SOEs out of strategic planning in a state monopoly sector. As a result, according to the logic of previous analyses, "disorganized despotism" cannot be properly applied to the Third Line Enterprises.

On the whole, due to the structural differences, neo-traditionalism and disorganized despotism are not applicable to the Third Line Enterprises. Moreover, previous studies also have one reductive problem. In their analysis, the management is assumed to be uniform and well-integrated, with the group leaders obedient to their upper level managers without any autonomy. Although, in discussion of the "broker" role of the group leaders, Walder has more or less identified the autonomy issue; he chooses to pursue a different path in his later discussion, for better or worse. In the analysis of neo-traditionalism, the group leaders are merely regarded as the clients of their senior managers, controlling group workers by establishing new patron–client ties with the activists. Do these group leaders completely follow their bosses in day-to-day production? If not, how do they find a balance between their bosses and their member workers? Walder's framework is not intended to answer these questions.

Fundamentally, this reductive problem is rooted in the assumption that the interest of group leaders fully overlaps with the interest of the organization. In Walder's work, the ultimate goal of urban SOEs is the political control of workers. As for firms of disorganized despotism, their only aim is to be at the top in the fierce market competition. However, these organizational goals are unlikely to be group leaders' primary concerns. In fact, as the organizational goals are disaggregated and transmitted to various departments and groups, it is necessarily the case that the interests of the groups deviate from those of the organization. The clear-cut and strict regulations demarcating the boundaries of leaders' responsibilities further encourage group leaders to prioritize their group interests, which now and then go against the interests of the organization as a whole. It is the existence of such local and departmental interests that give rise to the well-known "managerial dilemma" (Miller 1992). The interest of group leaders should therefore not be taken as exogenously given and defined by their top leaders. Rather, it is more plausibly seen as endogenous of the group leaders' quotidian interactions with senior managers and the lower member workers. Simply put, it is defined by the group leaders' unique position in the organizational hierarchy of the factory. It is precisely from this position of power and the associated agency that group leaders gain their autonomy and develop their strategies and tactics in dealing with day-to-day production issues. As a result, without knowing how the group leaders—the only "managers" having immediate contacts with workers—maneuver their limited but influential power, it would be difficult to see the full picture of how day-to-day production issues are managed.

The simplifying assumption reveals the dichotomous logic of the conventional wisdom on Chinese industrial relations. Under this logic, workers are regarded as either obedient or defiant, while managers are either oppressive or compromising. In nature, this dichotomous analytical framework does not go beyond the Marxist perspective that labor and capital owners are in conflict and their interests are hard to reconcile. A prerequisite for this perspective is the convergence of interest within both classes, which is predetermined by their material status in the production. However, as discussed above, the management is fragmented and each segment seeks their own interests through daily interactions. In this respect, the industrial relationship is more likely a *mutually adaptive* than a *conflicting* one. The case of the Jinjiang Factory shows that this adaptation is conditioned by the factory's social structure and the workers' control over production. The aim of such adaptation is to achieve a consensus that can guarantee the group's production and at the same time meet its members' needs.

The review of previous studies calls for a more contextualized and inductive-based analysis. What are the contextual features of the Third Line Enterprises? Under these conditions, what agency do the group leaders have? I attempt to answer these questions in this book.

1.2   TOLERATION: A GOVERNING STRATEGY AS A RESULT OF CONTEXTUAL CONDITIONS

Facing workers' rule-breaking behaviors, such as taking a shower during working hours, being drunk at lunchtime, and so on, group leaders of Jinjiang Factory did not usually punish them or report them to their senior managers. Instead, they were inclined to exhibit tolerance. Why did they do so? In this book, I argue that the group leaders' toleration was an *adaptive* strategy cultivated by the factory's densely interconnected social networks and the workers' control on production lines in the isolated area.

The Interconnected Social Networks in Jinjiang Factory

Toleration was the group leaders' choice primarily because workers in the Jinjiang Factory were interconnected through a series of close-knit relationships. The Jinjiang Factory was located in Danjing Mountains in the region of Chengdu and covered 25.88 hectares. Bicycles and shuttle buses were the only modes of transportation linking the remote site to the outside world. Living in this self-sufficient isolated site, workers had to seek their friends and marital partners within the factory. As a result, the workers were connected to each other in one way or another. However, it is worth noting that the construction of relationships did not occur randomly, but in a particular pattern deeply embedded in the social composition of the workforce. In the Jinjiang Factory, workers were divided into three different groups: those transferred from the east coastal cities or provinces (*neiqian zhigong*), Returned Educated Youths (*fancheng zhiqing*), and demobilized soldiers (*tuiwu junren*). With some exceptions, members of each group were more likely to seek their marital partners within that group.

If workers in the Jinjiang Factory were separated into three main groups, is it possible that the production group leader would be able to patrol his/her member workers of a different origin more assiduously? Such inter-group competitiveness was rare, although not totally absent. The reason is that the workers' job niches in the factory were closely associated with their origins. For example, the demobilized soldiers occupied the Machining Workshop, while the transferred workers formed the overwhelming majority in the Instrument Workshop. In other words, workers and their production group leaders usually share the same background. This will be discussed in detail in Chap. 4.

To sum up, the boundary among different groups of workers was perceived and further solidified through the constant day-to-day interaction and different job niches in the factory. Eventually, these interwoven social relations to some extent informalized the formal relations and blurred the boundary between family and factory.

Workers' Control on Production in Jinjiang Factory

Group leaders were inclined to give their toleration also due to workers' weapons on the process of production. Fundamentally, these "weapons" were rooted in the workers' permanent employment status and their lack of job mobility within the factory. As the case of the Jinjiang Factory shows, workers usually stayed in a particular job and seldom moved to another one. In an emergency, workers might be transferred to help out in different workshops. However, such transfers were temporary. Upon completion of the required production tasks, the assisting workers would go back to their original positions. It is also worth noting that the lack of internal mobility not only served the factory's interest but also was welcomed by workers. An obvious reason for this is that productivity grows with proficiency. More importantly, it enabled the workers to exert control over their pace of work. Greater experience in one position equipped workers with better knowledge of the work, such as the process of material distribution, the condition of tools and machines, the personality of relevant colleagues, and so on. To workers, perhaps nothing is more valuable than this tacit knowledge of production. With such knowledge, they came up with three main methods to manipulate their time at work. First, they changed the sequence of processing between different parts; second, they recalibrated their work quota between different tasks; third, they made use of the lack of coordination between activity or plans of different departments, workshops, working groups, and even individuals to manipulate their working time. Shielded by their permanent employment status, workers took advantage of these "weapons" to gain leverage over their dealings with supervisors. Aware of these workers "weapons", supervisors were thus more willing to tolerate a certain level of workers' rule-breaking behaviors.

The foregoing discussion illustrates that toleration as a governing strategy should not be understood through a simple dichotomous framework in which toleration is simply regarded as a compromise of supervisors confronted by powerful workers. The story of Jinjiang Factory shows that the toleration was due not only to powerlessness but also to personal emotion. Embedded in the widening informal social circles, the group leaders seemed reluctant to enforce the formal rules strictly. The toleration was therefore more of an *accommodation/adaptation* than a *compromise* to a specific social context of Jinjiang Factory.

1.3   TOLERATION IN PRACTICE: THE GOVERNANCE OF ABSENTEEISM AS AN EXAMPLE

How did toleration manifest itself in daily management? In this section, I show that as a governing strategy, toleration was not a simple attitude. Rather, it referred to a systematic management means. In order to better illustrate the tolerating strategy practiced in Jinjiang Factory, I take the group leaders' management of workers' absence as an example. In this example, the tolerating strategy was implemented based on the following three building blocks: the reinterpretation of workers' absence, the exchange among multiple actors, and the tactics sustaining the exchange. There are good reasons for analyzing industrial relations through the phenomenon of absenteeism. First, non-attendance is the most common way of rule-breaking behaviors in the workplace; second, it is a social phenomenon embedded in the structural context of work organization; third, it represents a form of conflict indicating a set of workplace relations (Edwards and Whitston 1989).

The Reinterpretation of Workers' Absence

Usually, absence refers to a state of being away from duty without the factory's permission. In this sense, absence is rule-breaking behavior that should be avoided as much as possible. In Jinjiang Factory, however, workers' absences were reinterpreted and justified as an understandable individual exceptional circumstance. Since every worker had his or her share of exceptional circumstances, there should be no distinction between individuals and all should be treated equally. On the basis of this understanding, group leaders maintained their production through coordinating a give-and-take exchange between the absent worker and the other member colleagues.

The Exchange Among Multiple Actors

The simplest exchange involves three parties at the same time: the absent worker, the other colleagues in the group, and the group leader. Among them, the absent worker is the "taker", benefiting from the group leader's tolerance and his colleagues' assistance, while the colleague worker is the "donor", giving his/her help to the absent worker and the group leader. Therefore, in this exchange, the group leader is a coordinator, acting as both a taker and a donor. When a similar circumstance happens to the relief worker next time, the give-and-take relations will be reversed. This simplest exchange equilibrium is illustrated in Fig. 1.2 in which "➔" denotes "gives to".

The simplest form of the exchange is a typical reciprocal relationship in which the favor is returned to the same person who gives the help (Wasserman and Faust 1994). In practice, however, this typical reciprocal exchange does not usually happen. Instead, it often occurs in two more complicated ways. First, in the words of Ekeh (1974), it is the "chain gen-

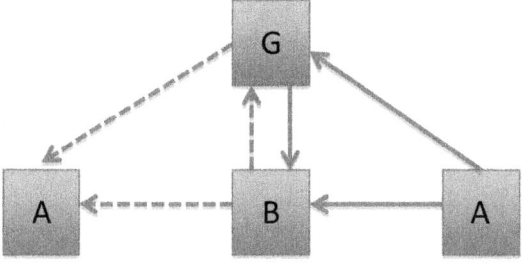

Fig. 1.2 Simplified equilibrium of the social exchange among multiple actors. (Note: In the exchange identified by the solid arrows, B is the absent worker and A is the donor of assistance, while in the exchange identified by the dotted arrows, the give-and-take relationships are reversed. "G" refers to the group leader)

eralized exchange". This form of exchange operates as follows: given five members (A, B, C, D, and E), A ➔ B ➔ C ➔ D ➔ E ➔ A, where "➔" denotes "gives to". In this exchange, each member will give his/her assistance to others. Even though he/she may not be able to receive help from the taker directly, he/she will certainly be repaid by others. Second, it is the "individual-focused net generalized exchange", which can be notated as follows: ABCD ➔ E; ABCE ➔ D; ABDE ➔ C; ACDE ➔ B; and BDCE ➔ A (Ekeh 1974). In this exchange, the donor is not a single person, but a collection of individuals. In the Jinjiang Factory, a typical example is the assistance given to demobilized soldiers for their farming work. Since most demobilized soldiers are also farmers in nearby counties, they have to go back home every spring and autumn for planting and harvest. To deal with their long-term absences, the group leaders usually motivate other member workers to provide help. Given that the demobilized soldiers account for almost one-third of the workforce, this is a common exchange in the Jinjiang Factory.

Of course, this managerial control cannot operate with group leaders' oral and spiritual support alone. They seek to accumulate two most crucial resources, money and time. This is done through the development of a set of tactics in day-to-day production.

The Tactics for Time and Money[2]

In order to carry out the exchange among members, group leaders need two resources in hand. For one thing, they must have enough "extra time" to be allocated to the absent workers for them to deal with the "exceptional circumstance"; for another, they also need some "extra money" to compensate the donors for their potential loss. In Jinjiang Factory, the group leaders seek to expand their allocable time in three ways: to selectively parcel out jobs to member workers; to cheat the attendance record; and to exploit "the time of waiting for jobs". To balance the economic interest among workers and compensate for their potential losses, they also invented three tactics. First, they build up the group private coffer; second, they initiate the trading of working hours between the absent worker and the donor; and, third, they adjust the time quota between different jobs. All these tactics are illegal under the factory's formal regulations because they prevent the factory from making full use of its workforce. However, they provide the supervisors a great deal of help in solidifying their members and completing their tasks. The factory and workshop managers, therefore, are in a dilemma because despite the *vicious* effects of these tactics, they have to admit the necessity of their existence. As a result, the factory management was always equivocal about these informal tactics.

The example of absence management reveals that the tolerating strategy implicitly indicated an egalitarian culture in the Third Line Enterprises. This egalitarianism does not come from nowhere; it is deeply rooted in the enterprise social context.

Despite the fact that the equity issue had appeared repeatedly in the official and factory managers' discourse, it was not a precept in daily governance in the mid-1970s. According to Walder's (1986) neo-traditionalism, in Chinese workplaces prior to the reform era, workers were basically divided into activists and non-activists. The activists, as the clients of their group leaders, usually enjoyed preferential treatment and benefits more than their member colleagues. In the 1980s, as a series of market-oriented reforms began in Chinese SOEs, the activists' advantageous position declined (Walder 1991). An unintended consequence of the reform was the rise of egalitarianism on the shop floor. As Walder reveals in his later work, shop directors and group leaders paid out bonuses relatively equally, rotated the high bonuses to different workers each month, and either neglected to set realistic individual quotas or ignored them at bonus time (Walder 1987).

To some extent, the shift of the factory's distribution scheme is a result of the increase of workers' bargaining power. In the mid-1970s, the party organization played an important role in controlling workers. The inspectorial role of activists and the politicized reward system are recognized as the core mechanisms of party discipline (Walder 1986). As a result, the workforce during this period was dependent on the management and an income differential is found between activists and non-activists. In the early 1980s, the reform to "expand enterprise autonomy" released managers and workers from the tight restrictions of the previous system of central planning and party supervision (Whiter 1984). Still unable to freely dismiss individual workers or to reduce unilaterally the size of their labor force by laying off workers, managers over this period had to keep differences in bonuses to a minimum to win the cooperation and consent of labor (Walder 1987). In the words of Gallagher (2005), it was "a new dependence of managers on their workforce".

In view of the previous analysis, the egalitarian governing strategy in the Third Line Enterprises can also be seen as a result of powerful workers.

As mentioned above, the interconnected informal relations in the factory reduced the influence of the formal regulations; the workers' control on production provided them with diverse ways to express their discontent. As a result, the group leaders in Jinjiang Factory treated their member workers' exceptional circumstances in an unexceptional way.

1.4   Informants and Interviews

The empirical evidence for this book comes mainly from in-depth interviews with former workers of Jinjiang Factory. My fieldwork was undertaken between mid-March and mid-July 2013. In December 2013 and January 2015, I conducted two rounds of follow-up interviews in Shanghai and Chengdu. Overall, I gathered information from 55 informants, consisting of 42 former workers of Jinjiang Factory, 3 officials and 10 scholars studying similar topics. This section details the whole process of my fieldwork in four subsections. The first subsection introduces how I gained access to the hidden Third Line workers. The second subsection deals with the issue of how informants were selected. The diverse profile of the subject pool ensures a degree of external validity. The third subsection describes how the interviews were conducted and the methods employed to reduce the informants' scope for giving self-serving answers. The last subsection provides a brief introduction to the supplementary sources of data, which includes local chronicles, factory documents, factory chronicle, personal memoirs, working diaries, and conference minutes.

Gaining Access to the Third Liners

To obtain first-hand information on the internal dynamics of Third Line Enterprises, the best way is to have direct access to such an enterprise and talk to its workers. Unfortunately, since anything related to the Third Line Construction used to be a top-level national secret, little information has been released and openly discussed through official channels. Even today, these enterprises remain unknown to most Chinese people. The mystery of the Third Line Enterprises challenged this study from the very beginning. As a first attempt, I typed "三线企业" (Third Line Enterprises) and "三线工人" (Third Line workers) into Baidu, the most popular Chinese search engine, in the hope of finding some clues about these mysterious and probably forgotten people. As I carefully scrolled down the webpage and filtered through the useless search results, a link named "锦江厂人吧" ("Post Bar of Workers of Jinjiang Factory") suddenly caught my eye.[3] I was exhilarated at this good luck, but little did I know at that time that this factory would become the center of my life in subsequent months.

Selecting Informants

Since the subjects of this study were difficult to locate, snowball sampling was the most practical method of recruiting informants. I contacted a small number of initial informants through the abovementioned "Post Bar of Workers of Jinjiang Factory". Before I left Singapore, I posted a message headed "A Student Asking for Help from Workers of Jinjiang Factory". This message contained my biography, the aim of my study and my contact details. It did not take me long to get in touch with two workers who expressed their willingness to offer help. Although many other respondents did not promise any direct help, they invariably recommended a name, Ni Tongzheng. Before I had a chance to email him, Mr. Ni contacted me and asked a series of detailed questions about my citizenship and educational background, and the topic, aims, and outline of my study. After making sure that I was not a foreign spy intending to probe the former national secret, he accepted my request and agreed to help.

When I arrived in Chengdu, Mr. Ni was waiting for me at the railway station. At the Wukuaishi Bus Interchange, we boarded a bus bound for Pengzhou, the county-level city where Jinjiang Factory is located. After traveling for an hour by bus and another 15 minutes by taxi, we arrived at Mr. Ni's home. He generously expressed his willingness to provide me with accommodation for the following days. The chance to eat and live with research subjects is undoubtedly valuable and helpful to any ethnographer. From a casual talk over lunch, I learned that Mr. Ni was a transferred worker from Shanghai. He used to teach at the factory's technical school and people therefore usually called him *Ni Laoshi* ("teacher Ni"). This form of address did not change even after he took up another post as director of the factory's General Office. In 1997, he took early retirement. Six years later, Jinjiang Factory went bankrupt. In memory of their beloved factory and the workers' dramatic yet little-known experiences, Mr. Ni motivated as many of his colleagues as possible to write their personal memoirs. By the end of 2013, Mr. Ni and his colleagues had completed three volumes of memoirs containing more than one million words and an album of more than 1600 photos.

It is Mr. Ni's rallying capacity and his extensive and effective personal networks that make him the best person to serve as the key initial informant. With his great help, I was able to enlarge and diversify the sample of informants. First, my informants had all held leadership positions at various levels. The bulk of the 42 informants working in Jinjiang Factory were production workers (14) and work group leaders (12). Meanwhile, I was also able to interview workshop and factory leaders. Table 1.1 reports the number of informants holding various positions.

Second, my informants were also diversified in terms of their personal backgrounds. Eighteen were transferred workers, accounting for the largest proportion of informants. Of the rest, 12 were Returned Educated Youth, 8 were demobilized soldiers, and 4 belonged to none of these three groups. Third, my informants worked at a wide range of departments. Though the majority worked in workshops, I did manage to interview some workers who worked in the transportation and quality control department (Table 1.2).

In addition, the interviews also included a handful of officials and scholars. In December 2013, I had a chance to interview three govern-

Table 1.1   Distribution of informants in different positions

Position	Number
Factory Management	7
Workshop Director/Party Branch Secretary	5
Section Chief	4
Group Leader	12
Production Worker	14
Total	42

Note: The "Factory management" includes two vice factory directors, four directors and vice directors of the factory general office, and one member of staff in the department of quality control

Table 1.2   Distribution of informants in different departments

Department	Number
Machinery Workshop	13
Heat Treatment Workshop	6
Instrument Workshop	5
Matching Parts Workshop	10
Quality Control Department	1
General Office	4
Factory Directorship	2
Truck Convoy	1
Total	42

ment officials who had participated in the Third Line Construction. Even though they were not able to provide any specific knowledge on workshop production, their personal experiences contributed considerably to my understanding of the broader background to this national project. I also conducted some informal interviews with scholars who shared my research interest. Among the ten scholar informants, two focused on the macroindustrial policy and the other eight, like me, studied the micropolitics within factories in Chongqing, Guizhou, and Yunnan. By exchanging our observations in different regions, I had greater confidence in the generalizability of the case under study. I obtained access to these officials and scholars via two channels. First, I searched for them online and exchanged emails with them. Second, when I participated as a presenter at "The Second Annual Conference on the Third Line Study" held at Shanghai University in December 2013, I met and talked to a few officials and scholars in person.

The Interviews

During my fieldwork in Pengzhou and Shanghai, Mr. Ni was not only my invaluable initial informant but also my indispensable research assistant. He made initial telephone contact with every intended informant, took me to the interview venue and warmly introduced me to his colleagues. In almost every interview, he sat on one side taking notes with me and, at the same time, frequently intervened to interpret some tricky dialects—and, from time to time, refilled everyone's tea.

Almost every formal interview had to start with a clarification about me, not just an introduction. Although Mr. Ni had already introduced me to the informants and explained the main focus of my research over the phone, the interviewees were still very curious as to why a young man would bother to come to a remote area to study an event that had occurred decades before. This usually led to a discussion of my family life, my research and career motivations, and how I got involved in this topic in the first place. No matter what they asked about me, I spared no effort in explaining things to their satisfaction. My open attitude and sincere disposition were crucial in building an excellent rapport and trust between us. I also explained to them that the interviews would be completely confidential and that I would not record their voices using any electronic devices. When these invited interviewees were satisfied with my accounts they gave their consent to the interview, and I moved on to the specific questions.

The interviews were not based on fixed questionnaires but were semi-structured sessions. Walder (1986, pp. 263–64) once said that "informants unfailingly illuminated additional, sometimes quite unexpected, dimensions of factory life, and this meant that new questions inevitably arose in the course of an interview". The same thing happened in the course of my interviews. As a result, as time passed, my interview questions evolved a lot and became more and more comprehensive and targeted. Basically, I divided my questions into four broad sections corresponding to four topics. The first was the interviewee's personal career history, which referred to the type of work, pay levels, why and how they joined the Third Line Enterprises, and so on. The second section comprised questions on their daily life outside the workshops. In this section, interviewees were asked to recall how they spent their leisure time, how they made friends and got married, and how they made their living in such an isolated area. The third section mainly concerned workers' lives in the workshops. I enquired about their routine process of production, relations with colleagues and leaders, how they speeded up or slowed down the pace of work, how they dealt with inspection by senior management, how bonuses and honors were distributed in the group, and so on. This was usually the largest section. The final section contained questions on connections with the outside world. For example, how often did they go to the nearest village market? Under what conditions were they allowed to go back home? Could they find their marital partner in the nearest village or not? Did they recruit any temporary farmer workers?

In practice, however, the informants' accounts often did not flow smoothly, which made it impossible to structure the interview sequentially in terms of the four sections. Therefore, as I noted their answers, I also marked the missed questions or topics and brought them up in an appropriate stage. Many times, the informants were so talkative and flexible that they led the conversation in irrelevant directions. However, unlike many other interviewers who would, perhaps, immediately steer the conversation back to the original topic, I just let the informants go on. Sometimes I even joined these seemingly irrelevant discussions until they finished the digression themselves. I did this for two reasons. First, I did not want to make them feel offended by forcing them to stop a topic they were highly interested in. Second, the irrelevant topics sometimes brought about surprises. The informants' memory was like an unexploited mine. It is hard to predict when and where we can find our treasures. Every time a new piece of information was brought to light, I would keep probing until it was fully extracted. This is why it always took me four to five hours to conduct an interview.

A common problem faced by fieldworkers is how to know whether informants are telling the truth (Dean and Whyte 1969). It is believed that informants always give self-serving interpretations of events and practices (Van Maanen 1983). As a result, the credibility and reliability of the interview are compromised. In order to lessen this problem, "triangulation" is usually recommended. The basic premise of triangulation is that one can be more confident about a result if it can be verified across two or more sources or methods. To employ this method in field research, "the most important [thing] is the ability to interview many people about the same event or institution" (Walder 1986, p. 256). As discussed above, the key informants came from the same factory and lived in the same place; therefore, triangulation can be readily employed in this study. Generally speaking, this study uses triangulation in three ways: first, to compare the responses of different informants to the same event and topic; second, to compare the responses of the same informants in the first and subsequent rounds of interviews; and, third, to compare the responses of informants with conference notes, working diaries, and completed personal memoirs.

Other Sources of Data

In addition to the interviews, this study also relies on the following supplementary sources to substantiate the argument.

First, the Local Chronicles of Sichuan and Chengdu, especially the volume on the machinery industry, provided me with tremendous information on the history of the Third Line Construction in this region. They were borrowed and read in the National Library of China in Beijing. Second, factory documents were collected from the abandoned workshops and the Office of Retirement Services (*tuixiu guanli zhan*), the only remaining organization of Jinjiang Factory, which is responsible for basic civilian services for the retired workers. These documents contain a lot of information on the daily operation of the factory and the workshops. Third, the Factory Chronicle—received from Mr. Ni—introduced me to the whole history of Jinjiang Factory, which included much valuable information on the factory's organization, workforce profile, key products, and so on. Fourth, Mr. Ni also gave me the three volumes of memoirs, which considerably enriched my knowledge of the workers' daily life. Fifth, some workers also generously donated their conference minutes and working diaries to support my study. These precious manuscripts record many of their life fabrics from the late 1970s to the mid-1990s, although not in great detail. Events are recorded in point form rather than narrative. Although these documents cannot provide any detailed information about a particular event, they are nevertheless useful for other purposes. For example, the meeting minutes and diaries allowed me to calculate how often a particular issue was raised. If one issue repeatedly appeared in the factory's conference minutes, this is a clear indication that it was not a trivial one that could be ignored in the factory.

1.5   Overview of the Book

This book consists of eight chapters. Chapter 2 briefly introduces the background to the Third Line Construction and Jinjiang Factory in comparison with seven other key construction projects of the Chengdu machinery industry. Chapter 3 demonstrates the isolated situation of Jinjiang Factory. Specifically, the Third Line Enterprises are like "isolated islands" hidden in mountainous areas. Living and working in a high degree of isolation, the workers are dependent on the factory not only for acquiring the basic economic, political, and social necessities but also for constructing day-to-day social networks (friendship and marriage) through the multifarious daily entertainment activities and a series of reciprocal interactions. Chapters 4 and 5 further explain why the group leaders do not strictly enact the regulation and are more likely to tolerate the workers' rule-breaking behaviors. I argue that the toleration is due to the factory's interconnected social structure (Chap. 4) and the workers' control over the production (Chap. 5). Taking the control of absenteeism as an example, Chaps. 6 and 7 present how the group leaders' toleration manifests in day-to-day practice. Chapter 6 shows the phenomenon of absenteeism in Jinjiang Factory. Chapter 7 presents how the toleration, as a strategy of controlling, operates in governing absenteeism. Chapter 8 concludes with a summary of the findings and a brief reflection on two themes widely discussed in the existing literature, namely the varieties of industrial authority and relations between the organized dependency and the workers' natural obedience.

NOTES

1. The First Line refers to the border land and the coastal area, the Second Line is the area between the First Line and the Third Line. The Big Third Line refers to the investment and construction in the central and western provinces, while the Small Third Line refers to the investment and construction in the central and western areas within the provinces of the First and the Second Line.
2. These tactics suggest that the slack resource is necessary for exchange. Indeed, many scholars have already studied this phenomenon. However, the purpose here is not to show the author's originality on this phenomenon but to present that in what forms this phenomenon existed in the Third Line Enterprises. More importantly, this is an indispensable content in this study illustrating how the tripartite exchange could be sustained. As for studies relevant to the role of slack resource in the Chinese factory's management, see, for example, Lin 2011; Walder 1987. For the role of slack resource in other countries, see, for example, Lupton 1963; Pravda 1979.
3. The address of the post bar is http://tieba.baidu.com/f?kw=%BD%F5% BD%AD%B3%A7%C8%CB&fr=ala0.

REFERENCES

Blecher, Marc J. and Gordon White. 1979. *Micropolitics in Contemporary China: A Technical Unit During and After the Cultural Revolution*, Armonk, NY: M.E. Sharpe.

Blecher, Marc. 1997. *China Against the Tides: Restructuring Through Revolution, Radicalism and Reform*, London: Pinter.

Bachman, David. 2001 (June). Defence Industrialization in Guangdong, *The China Quarterly*, 166:273–304.

Bramall, Chris. 2009. *Chinese Economic Development*, London and New York: Routledge.

Chan, Roger C. K. et al. 1996. *China's Regional Economic Development*, The Chinese University of Hongkong Research Monograph No. 30. Hongkong: Hongkong Institute of Asia-Pacific Studies.

Chen, Donglin. 2004. The Great Adjustment of the Third Line Construction After the 1980s, *The Review of Party History*, 5:4–11.

Cai, Yongshun. 2006. *State and Laid-Off Workers in Reform China: The Silent and Collective Action of the Retrenched*, London: Routledge.

Dean, John P. and William F. Whyte. 1969. How Do You Know if the Informants Is Telling the Truth? in McCall and Simmons, eds. *Issues in Participant Observation*. Addison-Wesley Publication Com, 105–14.

Dong, Baoxun. 2001. A Historical Analysis of the Origin of the Third Line, *The Journal of Shandong University*, 1:89–93.

Ekeh, Peter P. 1974. *Social Exchange Theory: The Two Traditions*, London: Heinemann Educational Books Ltd.

Edwards, Paul and Collin Whitston. 1989 (March). Industrial Discipline, the Control of Attendance and the Subordination of Labor: Towards an Integrated Analysis, *Work, Employment and Society*, 3:1–28.

Frazier, Mark W. 2002. *The Making of the Chinese Industrial Workplace: State, Revolution, and Labor Management*, Cambridge: Cambridge University Press.

Gallagher, Mary Elizabeth. 2005. *Contagious Capitalism: Globalization and the Politics of Labor in China*, Princeton and Oxford: Princeton University Press.

Henderson, Gail and Myron S Cohen. 1984. *The Chinese Hospital: A Socialist Work Unit*, New Haven and London: Yale University Press.

Lin, Xi and Yin Ji. 1987. A Big Economic Stage, *People's Daily*, May 24:1.

Lupton, Tom. 1963. *On the Shopfloor: Two Studies of Workshop Organization and Output*, Oxford: Pergamon Press.

Lu, Feng, 1989. Danwei: A Unique Form of Social Organization, *Chinese Social Science*, 1:71–88.

Li, Hanlin. 1993. China's Danwei Phenomenon and the Mechanisms of Conformity in Urban Communities, *Sociology Research*, 5:23–32.

Lü, Xiaobo and Elizabeth J. Perry. (eds.) 1997. *Danwei: The Changing Chinese Workplace in Historical and Comparative Perspective*, Armonk, NY: M.E. Sharpe.

Lee, Ching Kwan. 1999 (March). From Organized Dependence to Disorganized Despotism: Changing Labor Regimes in Chinese Factories, *The China Quarterly*, 57:44–71.

Li, Caihua and Dayun Jiang. 2005. The Lessons of the Big Third Line Construction, *Journal of Northeast University*, 4:85–91.

Lin, Kun-Chin. 2011. Enterprise Reform and Wage Movements in Chinese Oil Fields and Refineries, in Kuruvilla and etc., ed. *From Iron Rice Bowl to Informalization: Markets, Workers, and the State in a Changing China*, Ithaca and London: ILR Press, 83–106.

Liu, Yanxun. 2012. The Youth and Agedness of the Third Line People, *China Newsweek*, April 23:66–69.

Miller, J. Gary. 1992. *Managerial Dilemmas: The Political Economy of Hierarchy*, New York: Cambridge University Press.

Mel, Gurtov. 1993 (June). Swords into Market Shares: China's Conversion of Military Industry to Civilian Production, *The China Quarterly*, 134:213–240.

Meng, Tao. 2013. The Spatial Change, Structural Adjustment and the Cluster Innovation of Enterprises in the Third Line Areas, *Reform*, 1:35–40.

Naughton, Barry. 1988 (September). The Third Front: Defence Industrialization in the Chinese Interior, *The China Quarterly*, 115:351–386.

Naughton, Barry. 1997. Danwei: The Economic Foundations of a Unique Institution, in Lü, Xiaobo and Elizabeth J. Perry, eds. *Danwei: The Changing Chinese Workplace in Historical and Comparative Perspective*, Armonk, NY: M.E. Sharpe.

Pravda, Alex. 1979. Spontaneous Workers' Activities in the Soviet Union, in Kahan, Arcadius and Blair A. Rubles, eds. *Industrial Labor in the USSR*, New York: Pergamon, 333–66.

Solinger, Dorothy. 1997. The Danwei Confronts the Floating Population, in Lü, Xiaobo and J. Perry Elizabeth, eds. *Danwei: The Changing Chinese Workplace in Historical and Comparative Perspective*, Armonk, NY: M.E. Sharpe, 195–222.

Van Maanen, John. 1983. The Fact of Fiction in Organizational Ethnography, in Van Maanen, John, ed. *Qualitative Methodology*, Beverly Hills, CA: Sage Publications, 37–55.

Walder, Andrew G. 1986. *Communist Neo-Traditionalism: Work and Authority in Chinese Industry*, Berkeley: University of California Press.

Walder, Andrew G. 1987 (March). Wage Reform and the Web of Factory Interests, *The China Quarterly*, 109:22–41.

Walder, Andrew G. 1991 (September). Workers, Managers and the State: The Reform Era and the Political Crisis of 1989, *The China Quarterly*, 127:467–492.

Whiter, Gordon. 1984. Changing Relations Between State and Enterprise in Contemporary China: Expanding Enterprise Autonomy, in Maxwell, Neville and Bruce McFarlane, eds. *China's Changed Road to Development*, Oxford: Pergamon Press, 43–60.

Womack, Brantly. 1991 (June). Transfigured Community: Neo-Traditionalism and Work Unit Socialism in China, *The China Quarterly*, 126:313–332.

Wasserman, Stanley and Katherine Faust. 1994. *Social Network Analysis: Methods and Approaches*, Cambridge: Cambridge University Press.

Yang, Mayfair Mei-hui. 1989. Between the State and Society: The Construction of Corporateness in a Chinese Socialist Factory, *Australian Journal of Chinese Affairs*, 22:31–60.

Yuan, Guofeng. 2003. The Adjustment and Reorganization of the Third Line Industries Are Almost Done, *People's Daily*, December 4:6.

Zhao, Minghua and Theo Nichols. 1996 (July). Management Control of Labor in State-Owned Enterprises: Cases from the Textile Industry, *The China Journal*, 36:1–21.

Zhou, Xueguang. 1999. Review on the Studies of Institutional Change of Chinese Organizations in Western Sociology, *Sociology*, 4:26–43.

CHAPTER 2

The Third Line Construction and Jinjiang Factory

2.1 THE THIRD LINE CONSTRUCTION

From the early 1960s to the late 1970s, a large-scale migration occurred in mainland China, as a result not of the Cultural Revolution but a massive program of investment in the region of central and western China, which is known as "the Third Line" (*sanxian*).[1] Figure 1.1 shows in detail the area of the Big Third Line Construction, which ranges from the east of Wushao Mountain to the west of the Beijing–Guangzhou Railway, and from the south of Yanmenguan, Shanxi to the north of Shaoguan, Guangzhou. This area covers the provinces of Gansu, Qinghai, Ningxia, Guangxi, Guizhou, Sichuan (including Chongqing), Yunnan, Shanxi, Hunan, Shaanxi, Hubei, Henan, and Guangdong (Yuan 2002).

This extremely influential development investment is recognized as the central government's response to a perceived external threat (Naughton 1988). After the collapse of its alliance with the Soviet Union in 1958, China faced a potential threat from either or both superpowers. Without any conceivable assistance from either, China was left on its own in facing the non-stop invasion and harassment by other hostile powers. Backed by American power, the Kuomintang had never given up its plan of a counterattack on the mainland. Meanwhile, India also stirred up the border conflict in western China, which soon escalated into military conflict. Moreover, the escalation of the war between Vietnam and the US in 1964 exacerbated the central leaders' anxiety. Given that China's major industrial capacity and population was concentrated in a few eastern and

© The Author(s) 2018
C. Chen, *Toleration*, New Perspectives on Chinese Politics and Society, https://doi.org/10.1007/978-981-10-8941-1_2

northeastern cities, it was imperative to develop an alternative industrial base to maintain production in the event of war. In the cover note of Guangdong's report on Third Line initiative, Mao's concluding comment is that "if we do not act now, it will cause immense sorrow in the future" (Mao 1996).

Indeed, the distribution of China's industrial capacity and population concentration was extremely uneven at that time. Northwestern China (including the Autonomous Region of Inner Mongolia) accounted for 45% of the Chinese land area, but only 5% of total national industrial output; the southwestern, including the provinces of Sichuan, Yunnan, Guizhou, and Tibet, only produced 6% of total national industrial output, while nevertheless accounting for 23% of the land area. In these two vast areas, there were only about 300 industrial and mining factories, most of which were in the light industrial and repair sectors. Moreover, throughout western China, railways remained non-existent and highways had been seriously underdeveloped. As a result, this part of the country was almost completely cut off from the more developed east (Xie and Luo 1990, p. 69).

In order to balance the uneven distribution of industrial capacity and construct an alternative industrial base, the government initiated transfers on an enormous scale from east to west. Consequently, a huge number of factories and workers were relocated from the cities of the east coast and the northeastern industrial base, such as Shanghai, Tianjin, Beijing, and Shenyang, to remote areas in the west. Taking Shanghai from 1965 to 1973 as an example, in the course of the Big Third Line construction, 411 factories and 92,200 workers were transferred to Sichuan, Guizhou, Shaanxi, Gansu, Qinghai, and Yunnan (Institute of Contemporary Shanghai Study 2007). Of these, 195 factories and 46,000 workers were in the mechanical engineering sector; 46 factories and 8400 workers were in meter and telecommunications; 29 factories and 8500 workers in metallurgy; 44 factories and 8000 workers in chemicals; 32 factories and 9300 workers in textiles; and 32 factories and 6800 workers in light industry (Sun 1990, p. 469). These "migrant workers" were tasked with at least two missions: to create an entire industry, beginning with mining and energy, and to further develop the defense sector (Naughton 1988, pp. 356–60). Workers in non-military industries were usually moved to small and less important cities, some of which have today developed into larger and significant centers, such as Panzhihua in Sichuan province. Workers in the defense industry, under Mao's direction of "close to the mountains, dispersed and out of sight", were sent to remote villages or mountainous areas, isolated from the outside world. The nature of this hidden and isolated working environment can be seen in Fig. 2.1.

In addition to the workers transferred from various eastern cities, the composition of personnel in the Third Line Enterprises was gradually further diversified by the recruitment of Educated Youths who had returned to cities, demobilized soldiers, graduates of the factory's technical schools, and university graduates. However, diversified the workers in these enterprises might be, they were similar in one respect: they were supposed to be politically credible. Due to the political and strategic significance of the Third Line Enterprises in war preparation, every worker had to undergo

Fig. 2.1 Abandoned workshop of Jinjiang Factory. (Note: Author's pictures, March 26, 2013)

extremely strict political investigation. As one scholar of the Third Line Construction commented (Chen 2003):

> Anyone who belongs to any of the following categories is not allowed to transfer with his/her factory: one whose political background is landlord, rich peasant, reactionary and rightist; one who has a grievance against the state repression on his/her lineal kin; one who is susceptible because of concealing serious political problems; one who has committed serious embezzlement and theft; one who engages in any kind of illicit trading; [a] capitalist who holds the exploitative standing and one who has committed any other serious violations of law and discipline.

The pureness and high quality of those selected can be summed up succinctly by a popular saying in the early mobilization stage, "Good man, good horse and good sword and spear".

By the early 1980s, in the area of the Third Line Construction, more than 1100 industrial projects had been completed (Yuan 2003), about 29,000 enterprises established (Lin and Ji 1987), and the number of Third Line workers had reached 16 million, which constituted one-third of the total number of workers in SOEs (Lin and Ji 1987). Among the Third Line workers, nearly four million were "migrant workers" (Liu 2012). Even though there has been no official release of detailed data on financial investment during the Third Line Construction, probably due to its high sensitivity in the past,[2] scholars estimate that the total capital investment was no less than 200 billion yuan (Meng 2013; Lin and Ji 1987). Xie reports the capital component of the Third Line program as a proportion of total national construction for each of the Five-Year Plan periods (Table 2.1) (Xie 1981).

In the late 1970s and early 1980s, China shifted its focus from military preparation to economic development. As a result, the top priority of the Third Line program ultimately faded away and the conversion of military industries began (Naughton 1988; Mel 1993). The purpose of this con-

Table 2.1 Third Line program capital as a proportion of total national construction

Year	%
1963–1965	38.2
Third Five-Year Plan (1966–1970)	52.7
Fourth Five-Year Plan (1971–1975)	41.1

version was to reallocate political, economic, and technical resources from military to civilian sectors, as well as to convert the unified military production system into an integrated military–industrial system (Commission on Science, Technology and Industry for National Defence 1990, p. 170; Frankenstein 1997). One component of the conversion was the restructuring of the Third Line industries. In November 1984, the Third Line Construction Adjustment Reorganization Planning Office of the State Council finally agreed on a plan to reform the Third Line Enterprises. An unspecified number of enterprises were closed or incorporated into others (Long and Cheng 1991, p. 2; Lin 1988, p. 2). Workers in remote villages and mountain areas were relocated for the second time.[3] By the end of 1996, 236 enterprises and institutions had left their original locations and moved to nearby small- and medium-sized cities based on the principles of proximity and economic suitability.[4] In addition, the local government in the new location took over control of these factories. For example, in 1985, 24 large factories, including electronics, optical instruments, precision machinery, and even nuclear engineering, were moved to Chongqing. Urban residency status was also returned to workers (Naughton 1988). Almost at the same time, 57 "Small Third Line" Enterprises owned by the Shanghai municipality and located in the mountain areas of Anhui Province were passed to the governors of Anhui and moved to different nearby cities (People's Daily 1987).

2.2   Jinjiang Factory: A Typical Third Line Enterprise

Jinjiang Oil Pump and Nozzle Factory is one of thousands of Third Line Enterprises. Its establishment was prepared in early March 1966 and construction was eventually completed in 1972. As my knowledge of Jinjiang Factory and the Third Line Construction accumulated, I realized that Jinjiang Factory was a typical Third Line enterprise, which might well serve as a representative case at least in the machinery industry.

First, Sichuan was the leading host province for the Third Line Construction. From 1964 to 1978, the government's financial investment in the Third Line Construction in Sichuan amounted to 33.505 billion yuan, of which 20.215 billion was from the central government's direct financial investment (He et al. 2003, p. 115). During this period, one-eighth of the total national industrial investment and a quarter of the total investment in the armaments industry went to this southwestern province (Xin 1999, p. 77). One hundred and seventeen factories and thousands of workers from the east coast and the northeastern industrial base were transferred here (The Committee of Local Chronicles of Chengdu 2010, p. 751).[5] Jinjiang Factory is one of them.

Second, Jinjiang Factory was Chengdu's key Third Line Construction project. By 1980, the accumulated government investment had reached 25.6 million yuan. Compared to the seven other key projects at the time, Jinjiang Factory was undoubtedly the largest and of greatest importance in terms of financial assistance from the government and size of workforce. Basic information on the key construction projects in Chengdu's machinery industry during this period is shown in Table 2.2.

Third, like other Third Line Enterprises, Jinjiang Factory was built in a concealed mountain area. Figure 2.2 indicates the exact location of the eight key construction projects. The smallest, thick circle at the center of the map indicates the entire urban area of Chengdu city in the 1960s, which was within the *yihuan* (literal meaning "the first ring") area of present-day Chengdu. Outside the urban area were vast stretches of farmland and rolling mountains. From this map it can be seen that, with the exception of the Hongqi Instrument and Meter Factory, all the key con-

Table 2.2 Key construction projects in the Chengdu machinery industry

Factory	Year of construction	Accumulated investment by 1980	No. of workers by 1989
Sichuan Gear Factory	1964	1643	3304
Chengdu Fittings Factory	1965	840	1633
Jinjiang Factory	1966	2560	2538
Minjiang Gear Factory[a]	1966	2148	–
Hongqi Instrument and Meter Factory	1966	379	634
Chengdu Hongqi Tractor Factory	1969	2063	2383
Sichuan Hongqi Diesel Engine Factory	1971	2144	2888
Chengdu Tractor-Operated Machine Factory	1971	134.5	–

[a]The Minjiang Gear Factory was merged with the Sichuan Gear Factory; the Chengdu Tractor-Operated Machine Factory was merged with the Chengdu Fork Truck Factory. As a result, there is no comparable record of their number of workers (The Committee of Chengdu Local Chronicles 1995, p. 15)

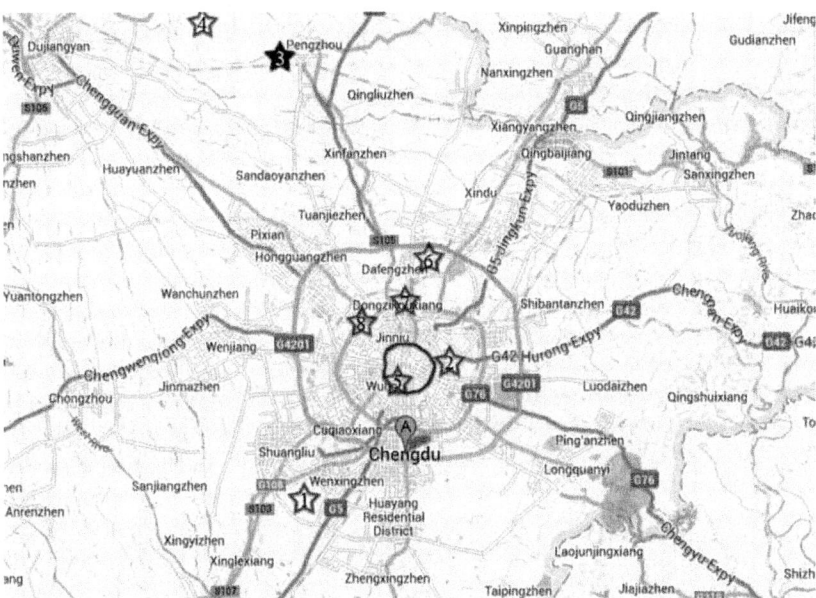

Fig. 2.2 Location of the key construction projects. (Note: Stars numbered 1 to 8 show the exact locations of the eight key construction projects: Sichuan Gear Factory, Chengdu Fittings Factory, Jinjiang Factory, Minjiang Gear Factory, Hongqi Instrument and Meter Factory, Chengdu Hongqi Tractor Factory, Sichuan Hongqi Diesel Engine Factory, and Chengdu Tractor-Operated Machine Factory, respectively)

struction projects were located far from the urban area of Chengdu, and even away from highways and railways. Jinjiang Factory, marked by the black star numbered 3, is one of the furthest from the city of these eight enterprises.

Fourth, unsurprisingly, transferred workers accounted for a large proportion of the workforce at Jinjiang Factory. Specifically, the transferred workers in Jinjiang Factory and the other seven factories were mostly from Wuxi Oil Pump and Nozzle Factory, Shanghai Baochang Piston Factory, Hangzhou Gear Case Factory, Tianjin Internal Combustion Factory, and Tianjin Tractor Factory, numbering in total around 1642 (The Committee of Chengdu Local Chronicles 1995, p. 14). The number of workers transferred by 1966 in these factories is given in Table 2.3.

Table 2.3 Number of transferred workers in key construction projects by 1966

Factory	Transferred workers by 1966
Sichuan Gear Factory	340
Chengdu Fittings Factory	156
Jinjiang Factory	444
Minjiang Gear Factory[a]	n/a
Hongqi Instrument and Meter Factory	n/a
Chengdu Hongqi Tractor Factory	n/a
Sichuan Hongqi Diesel Engine Factory	n/a
Chengdu Tractor-Operated Machine Factory	n/a

Note: n/a = not available

Source: *The Local Chronicles of Chengdu: The Chronicle of Machinery Industry*, pp. 14–21

[a]The Minjiang Gear Factory was merged with the Sichuan Gear Factory; the Chengdu Tractor-Operated Machine Factory was merged with the Chengdu Fork Truck Factory. As a result, there is no record of their number of workers by the year of 1989 (The Committee of Chengdu Local Chronicles 1995, p. 15)

In Jinjiang Factory, the personnel were even more diversified. By the early 1980s, there were 305 workers transferred from Shanghai Diesel Engine Factory, 137 from Wuxi Oil Pump and Nozzle Factory, 354 recruited from the technical schools of Shanghai Diesel Engine Factory and Shanghai Construction Mechanical Engineering Factory, 8 from the Eighth Machinery Ministry School of Industrial Accounting in Tianjin, 12 from Tianjin Agricultural Machinery Manufacture School, 35 from the Technical School of Luoyang Tractor Factory, 11 from Guizhou Diesel Engine Factory, and 5 recruited from Shanghai Xinhua Nurses School (The Office of Factory Chronicle 1986, p. 2). This is shown in graphic form in Fig. 2.3.

Last but not least, Jinjiang Factory's functional organizations appeared no different from others. The factory's multifarious organizations can be generally divided into three categories: production, logistics, and education. The production organizations constituted the largest share. According to *The Local Chronicles of Chengdu*, until 1989 the production system of factories in the machinery industry consisted of organizations in three layers: the factory headquarters, workshops, and groups. Large and medium-sized enterprises had an additional layer between workshops and groups called sections (The Committee of Chengdu Local Chronicles 1995, p. 226). As a large enterprise, Jinjiang Factory's production system had four layers. In the second layer, besides its 7 workshops, there were 22

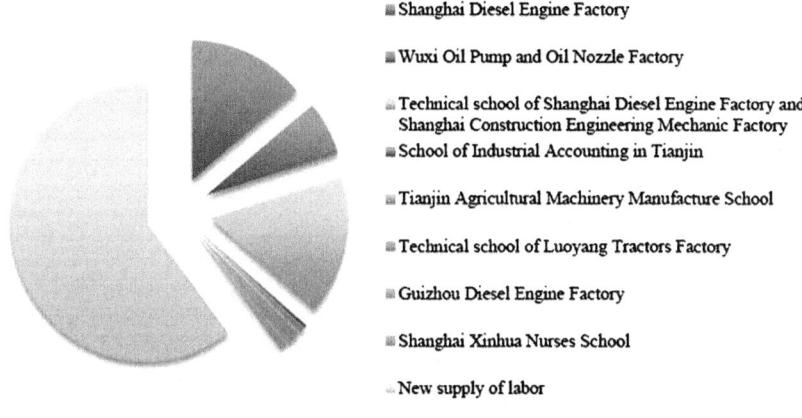

■ Shanghai Diesel Engine Factory

■ Wuxi Oil Pump and Oil Nozzle Factory

■ Technical school of Shanghai Diesel Engine Factory and Shanghai Construction Engineering Mechanic Factory

■ School of Industrial Accounting in Tianjin

■ Tianjin Agricultural Machinery Manufacture School

■ Technical school of Luoyang Tractors Factory

■ Guizhou Diesel Engine Factory

■ Shanghai Xinhua Nurses School

■ New supply of labor

Fig. 2.3 Composition of workers in Jinjiang Factory. (Source: The Office of Factory Chronicle, Jinjiang Oil Pump and Nozzle Factory, *Factory Chronicle: 1966–1985*, p. 2)

other departments administratively parallel to and functionally complementary with the workshops, such as the Sales Department, Design Office, and Quality Control Office. Figure 2.4 shows the organizational structure of Jinjiang Factory.

Overall, in comparison with the other seven enterprises in the machinery industry, Jinjiang Factory did not differ in any major respect. As a key project in Chengdu, the factory was concealed in the mountain area, made up of many transferred workers, and operated with multifarious organizations. It thus conformed to the typical template of Third Line Enterprises in almost all aspects. Although no single case can fully represent the whole picture, the typicality of Jinjiang Factory makes it at least a decent case to study.

As a significant economic program derived from direct political intervention, the Third Line Construction is undoubtedly a crucial event in China's industrial history. The assessment of its merits and demerits has already become a hot topic of scholarly debate. Yet, looking through the numerous existing literature on Chinese labor, few scholars have carried out a systemic study on Third Line workers so far.[6] The present study represents an effort to bridge this lacuna based on the experience of a typical Third Line enterprise, Jinjiang Factory.

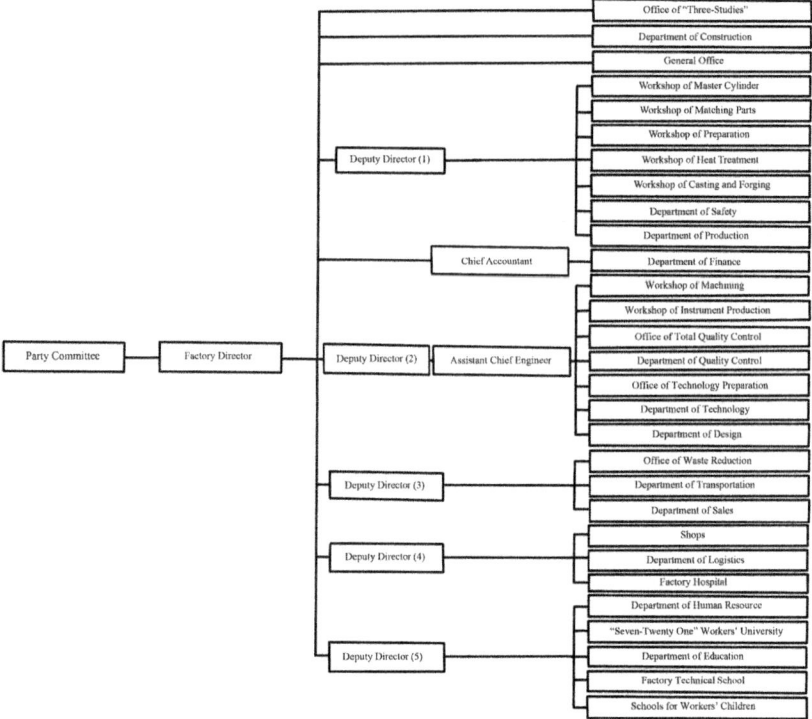

Fig. 2.4 Organizational structure of Jinjiang Factory. (Notes: (1) Following the reform of Factory Director Responsibility, the Factory Director no longer came under the Party Committee. Instead, the position sat alongside the Party Committee and took on total responsibility for production. The "7-21" Workers' University and "Office of Three Studies" were closed after 1978. (2) As shown in the diagram, there were five deputy directors in the Jinjiang Factory, each in charge of a different aspect of the factory's affairs. Deputy Directors 1–5 were respectively responsible for production, technology, operations, livelihood, and education and personnel matters; Source: The Office of Factory Chronicle, Jinjiang Oil Pump and Nozzle Factory, p. 28)

Notes

1. There are three recognized end dates of the Third Line program. Some argue for 1978, taking the Third Plenary Session of the 11th Central Committee as the mark; some opt for 1980, which marks the end of the fifth Five-Year Plan; while others contend that 1983 should be the end date

because in this year the central government finalized the policy for the adjustment and reorganization of the Third Line Enterprises (Li and Jiang 2005).

2. In "The Third Front", Naughton (1988) provides some estimated data on capital investment in the Third Line. David Bachman (2001) offers some estimates of the scale of Third Line investment in Guangdong province, while Ding (1997) gives some data on the conversion of Third Line industries in Guizhou province. All of them fail to provide any data on the scale of nationwide investment in the Third Line. Prior to the 1980s, there were no reports on the Third line Construction. According to the rules, copying any Third Line Construction documents was prohibited; neither could the term "Third Line" be used either orally or in writing. All information on the transfer of factories and workers was forbidden from being reported in newspapers, journals, and even in-house publications (Secrecy Committee of Shanghai, the Planning Committee of Shanghai and the Industrial Production Committee of Shanghai 1965).

3. Not all workers in remote mountain areas were relocated to nearby cities. Naughton (1988, p. 383) argued that "some factories gradually move out of the mountains by expanding into other locations...some factories have been dismantled and moved to nearby cities; some remain tied to raw material sources and struggle to succeed in production; and others have simply been abandoned".

4. Material-oriented processing companies moved to well-resourced cities such as Xiaogan (Hubei), Xianyang (Shaanxi), and Baoji (Shaanxi); companies producing appliances and goods for everyday consumption moved to highly populated cities such as Xiangfan (Hubei), Hanzhong (Shaanxi), and Mianyang (Sichuan); while high-tech companies moved to larger cities such as Wuhan (Hubei), Zhengzhou (Henan), Chongqing, Changsha (Hunan), and Chengdu (Sichuan) (Chen 2004).

5. There is no specific figure for transferred workers in Sichuan from 1964 to 1978. It is only recorded that in 1964 and 1965, 37,000 ordinary workers and technicians were transferred from the east coast area and the northeastern industrial base to Sichuan (the Federation of Trade Unions of Sichuan Province 1993, p. 34).

6. Nearly all works on the Third Line focus on the origin, scale, and legacy of this massive program. The "relocated workers" are not taken as their subjects. Studies on labor in China do not differentiate these workers from workers in other SOEs. William Hurst (2009) is one of the few scholars who took these workers as a group with a unique historical experience. Nevertheless, in his work he did not point out the scale of these workers.

REFERENCES

Bachman, David. 2001 (June). Defence Industrialization in Guangdong, *The China Quarterly*, 166:273–304.

Commission on Science, Technology and Industry for National Defence. 1990. *Survey of World Military Industry (Shijie junshi gongye gailan)*, edited by Science and Technology Intelligence Agency, Beijing: National Defence Industry Publishing House.

Chen, Donglin. 2003. *The Third Line Construction: The Western Development in the Period of War Preparation*, Beijing: The CCP Central Party School Publishing House.

Chen, Donglin. 2004. The Great Adjustment of Third Line Construction After the 1980s, *The Review of Party History*, 5:4–11.

Ding, Arthur S. 1997. The Regional Implications of Defence Conversion: The Case of the 'Third Line' and Guizhou, in Brömmelhörster, Jörn and John Frankenstein, eds. *Mixed Motives, Uncertain Outcomes: Defence Conversion in China*. London: Lynne Rienner Publishers, Inc., 135–149.

Frankenstein, John. 1997. China's Defense Industry Conversion: A Strategic Overview, in Brömmelhörster, Jörn and John Frankenstein, eds. *Mixed Motives, Uncertain Outcomes: Defence Conversion in China*, 3–34.

He, Haoju, et al. (eds.) 2003. *The Third Line Construction and the Western Development*. Beijing: The Contemporary China Publishing House.

Hurst, William. 2009. *The Chinese Worker After Socialism*, Cambridge: Cambridge University Press.

Institute of Contemporary Shanghai Study. (ed.) 2007. *The Memorabilia of Contemporary Shanghai*, Shanghai: Shanghai Lexicographical Publishing House.

Lin, Xi and Yin Ji. 1987. A Big Economic Stage, *People's Daily*, May 24:1.

Lin Rongqiang. 1988 (December 28). The First Case of Big Company Merger in Electricity Industry), *People's Daily*, 2.

Long, Xiangchao and Jian Cheng 1991 (December 04). The Adjustment and Reorganization of the Third Line Industries Has Achieved Great Progress, *People's Daily*, 2.

Li, Caihua and Dayun Jiang. 2005. The Lessons of the Big Third Line Construction, *Journal of Northeast University*, 4:85–91.

Liu, Yanxun. 2012. The Youth and Agedness of the Third Line People, *China Newsweek*, April 23:66–69.

Mel, Gurtov. 1993 (June). Swords into Market Shares: China's Conversion of Military Industry to Civilian Production, *The China Quarterly*, 134:213–240.

Mao, Zedong.1996. *Manuscripts of Mao Zedong Since the Founding of PRC, Volume 11 (1964–1965)*, Beijing: Central Party Literature Press.

Meng, Tao. 2013. The Spatial Change, Structural Adjustment and the Cluster Innovation of Enterprises in the Third Line Areas, *Reform*, 1:35–40.

Naughton, Barry. 1988 (September). The Third Front: Defence Industrialization in the Chinese Interior, *The China Quarterly*, 115:351–386.

People's Daily. 1987 (March 10). Anhui and Shanghai Remake 'Small Third Line' Enterprises, *People's Daily*, 2.

Sun, Huairen. (ed.) 1990. *A Brief History of Socialist Economic Development in Shanghai 1949–1985*, Shanghai: Shanghai People Press.

Secrecy Committee of Shanghai, the Planning Committee of Shanghai and the Industrial Production Committee of Shanghai. 1965 (February 5). *Circular on Enhancing the Confidentiality in Support of the Inner Land from the Secrecy Committee of Shanghai, the Planning Committee of Shanghai and the Industrial Production Committee of Shanghai*, Call no. A-38-2-792/104, Shanghai Archive, in Li, Hao. 2010. The Study on the Third Line Mobilization of Shanghai, (Master's thesis), retrieved from Dissertation and Theses Database of CNKI.

The Office of Factory Chronicle. 1986. *Jinjiang Oil Pump and Oil Nozzle Factory, Factory Chronicle: 1966–1985*.

The Federation of trade Unions of Sichuan Province. 1993. *The Chronicles of the Federation of Trade Unions of Sichuan Province*, Beijing: The Contemporary China Publishing House.

The Committee of Chengdu Local Chronicles. 1995. *The Local Chronicles of Chengdu: The Chronicle of Machinery Industry*, Chengdu: Chengdu Publishing House.

The Committee of Local Chronicles of Chengdu. 2010. *The Local Chronicles of Chengdu: Chronicle of Events*, Beijing: Fangzhi Publishing House.

Xie, Shirong. 1981. Military Industries Must Be Brought Fully into Play, *Review of Economic Research (Jingji yanjiu cankao ziliao)*, 59:33.

Xie, Minggan and Yuanming Luo. 1990. *Forty Years of Chinese Economic Development*, Beijing: People Press.

Xin, Wen. 1999. The Third Line Construction and the Establishment of Sichuan Industrial Base, in Wang, Chuncai, ed. *The Monument of the Third Line Construction*, Chengdu: Sichuan People Publishing House, 73–85.

Yuan, Li. 2002. *The Cluster Effect and the Cultivation of the Competitive Advantage of Western China*, Beijing: The Press of Economic Management.

Yuan, Guofeng. 2003. The Adjustment and Reorganization of the Third Line Industries Are Almost Done, *People's Daily*, December 4:6.

CHAPTER 3

The Context of Toleration (1): Isolated Life in Jinjiang Factory

Today, Ni laoshi (teacher Ni) introduced me to the vice director of the Jinjiang Factory, Yu Xuehui, and the Party Branch Secretary of the Heat Treatment Workshop, Tan Yi ... We walked in the rain for no less than 20 minutes and finally arrived at the downstairs of Yu's apartment. From outside the building, Ni laoshi shouted loudly, "lao Yu (old Yu)!" "Who is it?" asked Yu. "Me!" Ni replied.
From the author's fieldwork notes

Residing in a remote mountainous area, workers at Jinjiang Factory were isolated from the outside world. As a result, the factory was the only source of their economic, social, and political necessities. Moreover, it was the only circle within which they could establish their social relations. Living in this isolated factory and seeing almost the same group of colleagues for an extended period of time, Jinjiang Factory workers developed the ability to recognize each other merely by their voices. As in the case recorded in the author's fieldwork notes above, Mr. Ni did not even need to say his name for identification.

This chapter depicts the workers' isolated life in five respects. It starts with an introduction to the transportation connecting the Jinjiang Factory with Chengdu city. The second section discusses how the workers are supplied with enough food and drink. The third section details the factory's affiliated education units. The fourth section describes how the workers enriched their entertainment on their own in such an isolated area. The

© The Author(s) 2018
C. Chen, *Toleration*, New Perspectives on Chinese Politics and Society, https://doi.org/10.1007/978-981-10-8941-1_3

fifth section points out the workers' social interaction and social relationships in the factory. Specifically, due to the separation from kin and circles of friends in their hometowns, colleagues were the main source of workers' social support. As a result, Jinjiang Factory workers were in a reciprocal relationship and they established their social networks through friendship and marriage with their colleagues. Obviously, the workers' isolated life in the factory shows their high degree of organizational dependency. In order to distinguish the workers' dependency in the Third Line Enterprises from that of their urban counterparts and the rural collectives, in the final section, I make a broad comparison between these three different economic entities.

3.1   TRANSPORTATION

Following Mao's instructions, Jinjiang Factory was built in a concealed mountainous area. Specifically, it was situated on the mountainside in Longfeng Village, Peng County, administered by Chengdu city. In total, the factory occupied 25.88 hectares, almost evenly split into production and residential sites. The production site was located against the mountain facing the plain, running 400 meters east to west and 200 meters north to south. It consisted of three layers, the lowest of which was 700 meters above sea level. The residential site was located southwest of the production site, on a long and narrow slope, between 722 and 745 meters above sea level. The residential site was 50 meters wide and 700 meters long (The Office of Factory Chronicle 1986, p. 1). Figure 3.1 clearly shows that Jinjiang Factory was isolated and surrounded by mountains.

In this isolated area, a "shuttle bus" was the only vehicle connecting the factory with the nearby city. In the mid-1970s, Jinjiang Factory bought its first "shuttle bus" for its workers, "Liberation" (*jiefang*) truck. At 7 am every day, the factory's shuttle bus departed for Chengdu city. About one and a half hours later, it arrived at its destination, the North Chengdu Railway Station, and workers transferred to other modes of urban transportation as their individual needs required. Workers were usually given six hours to deal with personal matters in the city and had to return to the factory's shuttle bus at about 3 pm. Going back to the prosperous and lively city was enjoyable and attractive, but the three-hour round trip in the "shuttle bus" was a torture. Sitting in the truck's load-bed and holding on only to a hemp rope, workers struggled to balance themselves as the truck jolted and rattled over the rough mountain roads. Rain and wind

Fig. 3.1 Jinjiang Factory at Danjing Mountain. (Source: Author's photos, March 2013)

would make this experience even harder because the truck carrier was shielded only by a rippling canvas roof and sitting inside was therefore extremely uncomfortable in bad weather. Even though the factory's transportation was simple and crude, the service was actually not a free lunch. Throughout the 1970s, every passenger would be charged 40 cents for the round trip. This Liberation truck was in service for almost ten years. To improve its transportation capability, in the mid-1980s, the factory appropriated some funds from the technological transformation budget and bought two 45-seater coaches, one a Huanghai and the other a Huanghe.

The provision of the shuttle bus was also very helpful in satisfying the workers' needs beyond the immediate scope of the factory's service. For example, it could take workers to see the doctor in the event of serious illness, to buy clothes in department stores, to visit museum exhibitions, and so on. However, such special needs occurred only rarely and even when they arose and some workers needed to leave for cities, such trips first had to be approved by the factory. As a result, living in isolated mountain areas and with inconvenient transportation, Jinjiang Factory workers had to rely primarily on themselves within the factory to fulfill their daily living and entertainment needs.

3.2   FOOD AND DRINK

In addition to the state food ration, Jinjiang Factory and its workers sought many other ways to supplement their living. The provision of pork by the state was insufficient throughout the 1970s and the early 1980s. Fully aware of this situation, the factory built up a very good relationship with the Food Company of Peng County by offering several job opportunities in the factory for relatives of the company's leaders. In return, Jinjiang Factory gained the privilege of collecting its pork before the company's other customers. By so doing, the factory was able to deliver almost the best-quality pork to its workers. Moreover, thanks to the good relationship with the company's leaders, Jinjiang Factory could also gain some additional pork.

Vegetables were provided by three means. First, workers planted vegetables in some empty land in the factory's resident sites on their own initiative, such as garlic, spring onion, potato, and tomato. However, these self-planted vegetables were few in quantity and lacked variety, and so could only provide a marginal supplement to the workers' daily needs. By contrast, the vegetables provided in the periodic market in the nearby village were numerous and various. In this market, workers could buy not only vegetables and fruit but also eggs, chicken, honey, and many other foods for everyday consumption. As a result, going to this local market periodically became an important feature in the workers' lives. This activity was called, by the workers, *ganchang*. Besides the local market, there was actually a small vegetable market about 200 meters from the factory gate. This formed spontaneously, with some nearby peasants coming to sell their crops. Though this only partially met the workers' daily needs, it was indispensable to the workers living isolated in the mountain. As an interviewee recalled, "In those days, even though we all knew it [the small market] could be taken as the tail of capitalism, no one was willing to suspend it and it just continued to exist."

Since the workers at Jinjiang Factory came from many different regions, their dietary habits differed greatly. In order to satisfy the wide-ranging workers' dietary needs in such an isolated area, the factory had to diversify the food in the canteen and learn how to cook it. It assigned special workers to figure out how to make bean products, bread, mooncake, rice cake, and so on. The factory either allocated funds to buy the machines and tools necessary to make these dishes or just made them all by itself. For example, the oven and baking tray were designed and made by the factory's electrical engineer; the mold for making mooncake was made with the help of the director of the Machining Workshop; and the yeast for bread and buns was made by fermenting potato water. Through the efforts of the whole factory, workers were able to get access to the food of their hometown, even in this remote mountain area.

3.3   EDUCATION

Jinjiang Factory established its own schools to educate its workers' children. In 1972, the chief of the personnel section was assigned to take charge of the construction of the factory's affiliated primary and high schools. From their inception, these schools were reputable in Peng County. First, they acquired a local reputation for their high-quality teachers. Even though there were few teachers in these schools, their average educational background was above high-school degree level. Some of the teachers were even technicians or engineers in the factory with polytechnic or college degrees. Second, the schools were equipped with incomparable teaching devices and relevant support facilities. Laboratory apparatus and sporting equipment were all purchased in Shanghai. The schools were even equipped with a water filter system to provide students with safe drinking water. With such outstanding teachers and facilities, many students in these schools got good results in high-school and university entrance examinations.

Besides the primary and high schools, Jinjiang Factory also established its own technical school and "7-21" Workers' University.[1] The factory technical school recruited students who were not only the children of factory workers, but also qualified candidates from neighboring villages. The teachers were skillful workers with comparatively superior educational background. Usually, the students from the factory technical school were the main labor pool for the factory's annual recruitment. From 1976 to 1989, Jinjiang Factory Technical School recruited 688 students, of whom 648 graduated (The Committee of Chengdu Local Chronicles 1995, p. 215).

3.4   ENTERTAINMENT

As can be seen from Fig. 3.2, the production and residential sites were located close together in the Danjing Mountains, separated by the Longgui Road. The buildings marked 19 in the picture were the oldest workers' dormitory, the walls of which were made of timber, with clay used to seal gaps. Bricks were usually attached to the walls from the outside to consolidate the whole construction.[2] Shortly before 8 am every day, the factory loudspeaker played a tune that sounded exactly like the bugle call in the army. Its sound was loud enough to be heard in every corner of the factory, and it was usually at this time that workers poured out of their dormitories. Jinjiang Factory workers had good memories of this loudspeaker because it was not only a symbol of discipline but also an important channel of entertainment and emotional exchange (Fig. 3.3):

Fig. 3.2   The helicopter view of Jinjiang Factory. (Legend: 1 Front Gate; 2 Heat Treatment Workshop; 3 Instrument Production Workshop; 4 Matching Parts Workshop; 5 Master Cylinder Workshop; 6 Machining Workshop; 7 Laboratory Shop; 8 Casting and Forging Workshop; 9 Preparation Workshop; 10 Dining Hall; 11 Truck Convoys; 12 Warehouses; 13 5-7 Cooperative; 14 Kindergarten; 15 Back Gate; 16 Factory Hospital; 17 Lighting Courts; 18 Workers' Club; 19 Dormitories; 20 Longgui Road; 21 Dormitories; 22 Cinema; 23 Dormitories; 24 School for Workers' Children; 25 Factory Technical School; 26 Laboratory Field)

Fig. 3.3 Factory's back gate. (Source: Author's photo, March 21, 2013)

Even now, I can still clearly remember the sound of that loudspeaker. We started and ended our work to the bugle call every day. To us, it was just like a strict command. But actually, it also had some other functions. For example, to celebrate the birthday of a colleague, we usually ordered a song for him or her, with some spoken good wishes, of course. Sometimes, we even bought a cake![3]

The residential and production sites were connected by some zigzag gravel footpaths hidden under lush green vegetation. Sports and recreation facilities were located along these paths, as well as the eight workshops and other auxiliary production facilities. The football court was probably the largest open area in the factory. After the disbanding of the factory football team, this large area was subsequently transformed into several basketball courts. These courts could even be used at night, thanks to electric incandescent lamps hanging high above. It was precisely for this reason that Jinjiang Factory workers named it "the Lighting Court".[4] As long as weather conditions permitted, workers would come to this place for outdoor activities to relax at the end of the day's work. Some would pursue strenuous sports here, while others might come only to take a stroll.

Next to the court was the Workers' Club, a complex for indoor activities (marked 18 in Fig. 3.2). Here workers could read in the factory library and the periodicals room, exercise in the table-tennis room, play in the chess and card room, and relax in the TV room, art room, and even a karaoke room. Apart from the Lighting Court, the Workers Club served as the only functionally comprehensive place for workers to spend their daily leisure time.

Watching movies was an event of great interest that no one wanted to miss. Although they were not shown frequently, they did considerably enrich the workers' lives. News of an upcoming movie was always spread very quickly among workers, and on the release date the movie usually became one of the hottest subjects of conversation in the workshop during working hours. The cinema was thus another paradise in which workers could spend their spare time, though it was used much less than the Lighting Court and the Workers' Club (Fig. 3.4).

With these sports and entertainment facilities, Jinjiang Factory developed a range of group events (see Fig. 3.5). The many sport events were usually given high priority, among which the Annual Athletics Meeting was undoubtedly the foremost. The tug-of-war between two workshops was perhaps the event held most frequently, and it was also the favorite of

Fig. 3.4 Abandoned Lighting Courts. (Note: Author's photo, March 21, 2013)

Fig. 3.5 The third sports meeting of Jinjiang Factory

many workers. Moreover, volleyball, football, basketball, table tennis, and badminton matches, and even Chinese chess, for both men and women, were also frequently held. To make full use of the cinema, Jinjiang Factory also organized many cultural and artistic activities, such as singing contests, poetry-reading contests, and festival parties. The formation of Jinjiang Factory orchestra was another embodiment of the factory's enthusiasm for artistic events. Workers were very proud of their orchestra, which never failed to meet their expectations. The orchestra once won first prize in the Playing Competition among all the enterprises in the same industry in the entire region of Chengdu.

In addition, the factory also supported many events initiated by the factory-affiliated organizations. For example, every autumn, the Factory Workers' Children's School usually held a kite competition. Materials for making a kite, such as wire and cotton paper, were only available in some production workshops. Besides supplying materials, the factory workshops also made financial contributions to these activities. Because of the factory's involvement and support, activities for the children always served as activities for the whole factory. In his meeting minutes, Tan Yi wrote a brief record on the donation of each workshop for Children's Day.

> May 13, 1989. Fundraising Meeting for Children's Day
> Machining Workshop 280 workers, 280 yuan; Matching Parts Workshop A 220 workers, 220 yuan; Assembly Workshop, 100 workers, 100 yuan; Instrument Production Workshop 90 workers, 90 yuan; Forging and Casting Workshop 82 workers, 82 yuan; Heat Treatment Workshop 78 workers, 80 yuan; Preparation Workshop 57 workers, 57 yuan; Matching Parts Workshop B 198 workers, 200 yuan.
>
> Minimum Requirement: 1 yuan per person
> Actual Total Amount: 1240 yuan
> Allocation Plan: Workers' Children School, 800 yuan; Kindergarten, 300 yuan
> Balance: 140 yuan.

Thanks to the comprehensive recreational facilities, Jinjiang Factory workers did not live a boring life. They helped workers form a life in sharp contrast to the surrounding rural areas. Some may argue that the activities held in Jinjiang Factory could be also found in other urban factories. It is true enough that, in terms of the type of activities, there might not be a vast difference between Third Line Enterprises and urban factories. What distinguished the former from the latter, however, was the accessibility of the alternatives. For the Third Line workers in remote mountain areas, the factory site was almost the only place they stayed in and their factory colleagues were the only people with whom they could form social relationships. As a result, the life of workers and the structure of the working class in Jinjiang Factory were fundamentally shaped by the workers' frequent interactions with the same group of people in an isolated location.

3.5   Social Interaction and Social Relationship

A typical feature of Third Line workers was their separation from their kin and previous circles of friends. As a result, whenever they encountered any type of emergency, their factory colleagues were the only people they could turn to for help. In other words, colleagues, rather than their relatives, were the main source of workers' social support. Workers at Jinjiang Factory were thus in a reciprocal relationship with their colleagues.

Many scholars have argued that workers in urban factories were also living in a relatively closed system. Each enclosed unit was like an independent island in the city, separated from the others. Members of the unit were in a quasi-ethical relationship with the organization and their immediate colleagues. In almost all the factories, a system for conveying sympathy was well established when accidents of any kind occurred. Subjected to these special considerations, workers in urban factories were able to mentally and physically enjoy the corporate assistance to some extent. But this corporate assistance should not be exaggerated. According to an interview conducted by Henderson and Cohen in a socialist hospital of Wuhan, members of the hospital insisted that the social meaning of the work unit was nothing but an administrative designation (Henderson and Cohen 1984). It was people's ties to their traditional seat of family and kinship that played the dominant role in their social life. Indeed, though workers in the city were allocated to different work units, they had never been cut off from their kin and previous circle of friends.

The situation of workers at Jinjiang Factory was exactly the opposite. Even many local Sichuan workers were far from their birthplaces, not to mention those workers transferred from the eastern and northeastern provinces. Moreover, many of the workers recruited were young unmarried men and women in their early 20s. As these young workers gradually got married to each other in the factory, the social structure of the Third Line factories was characterized by nuclear families. At the time of the bankruptcy of Jinjiang Factory, about 30 years after its establishment, not a single family had three generations living under one roof except for a few transferred technicians who were much older than the others.

Living first as atomized individuals and then in nuclear families, workers felt a strong and persistent need to acquire help from their immediate colleagues. According to the experiences of workers in Jinjiang Factory, the need concerned almost every aspect of life, especially in an emergency:

> We were living together like a real big family. I remember once there was a female colleague who had a serious ectopic pregnancy problem. We sent her to the Peng County Hospital in the factory hospital's ambulance. On that day, she bled too much, and unfortunately there was not enough blood stored in the Peng County Hospital. It was already very late at night. I heard the loudspeaker broadcasting for a long time, emphasizing how dangerous

a situation our colleague was in and calling on us to have a blood test in the factory hospital and donate blood to find a match. At least more than a hundred people went to take the blood test.[5]

Of course this kind of life-and-death emergency did not occur often and certainly did not happen to everyone in the factory. But many workers would need to be accompanied when they were hospitalized. If a patient relied solely on their spouse, it would not only exhaust the spouse but also delay his/her production progress. Taking these real problems into account, the factory usually assigned some other workers to take turns to accompany the hospitalized patient with his/her spouse. For those who were assigned, all the hours spent looking after the patient would be counted as their working hours and they would be paid the hourly average wage of the whole workshop:

> In our factory, there was an unwritten rule that as long as someone was hospitalized and needed to be accompanied by our colleagues, every workshop must assign someone to shoulder the duty together with the patient's spouse. Actually, I was assigned once to accompany the head of the finance department. He fell ill with acute appendicitis and needed to be sent to Chengdu. His child was still very young at that time, so his wife definitely could not deal with this problem all by herself. All the expenses in Chengdu, including the trip and accommodation, could be reimbursed. Even more happily, the days I spent in Chengdu were counted as paid leave![6]

In Jinjiang Factory, some lucky demobilized soldiers whose home villages were located in nearby areas were envied much by others because they were able to get home in only one or two hours by bicycle. But this did not set them apart from the social relations in the factory. This group of people, in fact, received additional assistance from their colleagues. Every year during the rice transplanting and harvest seasons, every workshop would assign some workers to provide these demobilized soldiers with help in their farm work. The section chief in the Instrument Production Workshop, Huang Limin, explained the rationale of this assignment:

> Every spring and autumn, the demobilized soldiers would ask for leave for at least a week. We knew they had their farmland at home, and in these two busy seasons, they had to go back. But the problem was that some of these workers were in charge of key steps in the production process, or some of

them operated a machine that no one else could. As a result, the whole section might have to halt production merely due to the absence of one person. It was a dilemma, actually. At that time, unlike present private enterprises, you know, the factory could not freely fire workers. So we thought the only way to solve the dilemma was to help them complete their farm work as quickly as possible. That was why every workshop would send some workers to go home with the soldier worker. For those assigned workers, all their hours spent doing farm work would be counted as their working hours, and they would be paid at the hourly average wage of their workshop. Actually those demobilized-soldier workers also benefited from this arrangement. On one hand, they could finish their farm work in time; and on the other, they would not lose too much of their salary. In addition, through this process, we also hoped to strengthen the solidarity of workers in the same workshop.[7]

For the majority of workers at Jinjiang Factory, moving house was more frequent than one would expect. From single quarters to married quarters, and then to the nuclear-family quarters, every worker had to experience moving at least three times within five to ten years. In the course of each move, they were well assisted by their colleagues and the factory transportation facilities:

Our workshop was also responsible for assisting workers to move house. In Jinjiang Factory, every worker would experience moving several times. Small apartment, medium-sized apartment, medium-large apartment and large apartment … Every time the worker needed to move house, our workshop would assign some trucks and our colleagues to help us.[8]

The different types of social support listed above were by no means the whole picture of workers' life in Jinjiang Factory, but they may serve as an example of the broad reciprocal relations among workers. As a result of intensive contact over a long period, the Third Line Enterprises gradually evolved into an acquaintance society that was more like the traditional Chinese rural society. Workers living in this society, despite being away from friends and families in their birthplaces, were nonetheless able to restore their social relationships by making friends with and marrying their immediate colleagues. As Roger Gould once argued, "an unintended consequence of formal organizations … is the creation of social ties that encourage the recognition of commonalities on a scale considerably broader than would be expected on the basis of social networks alone"

(Gould 1995, p. 22). The social tie in Jinjiang Factory, as an unintended consequence, was widely created in the process of day-to-day entertainment and reciprocal interactions.

The effect of leisure activities on forging social networks has been mentioned repeatedly by social capital scholars. In an in-depth study of Shanghai's Bank of China in the early 1930s, Yeh found that the daily group sports and physical exercises such as tennis, ice hockey, horseback riding, basketball, and soccer played an indispensable role in strengthening the workers' solidarity (Yeh 1997). In this respect, workers at Jinjiang Factory were no exception. The various aforementioned entertainments within the isolated factory compound offered a platform for communication among the mixed group of people from all corners of the country. In the process, numerous subgroups among workers were gradually formed and strengthened. This was especially the case with team activities, such as basketball and volleyball, whereby friendships were relatively easier to form in the course of training and matches.

> In Jinjiang Factory, we made many new friends here. Take my experience as an example. Liu, Li, Tan, He and I were all working in the Heat Treatment Workshop. Even though we were working in different job positions, we usually played together in our leisure time. Sometimes we played basketball or badminton, and sometimes we played chess. Tan was really a big fan of chess! He even established a chess hobby group in the factory … In addition to the entertainment inside our factory, we also had some happy times together outside. Not far from Jinjiang Factory, there are some streams and brooks, where we occasionally went on Sundays to catch crabs, frogs, and eels. So Sunday was the time when our meals got better![9]

Chen's experience of making friends in the course of day-to-day activities was only part of the story. Besides friendship, bonds among Jinjiang Factory workers were also reinforced through marriage.

> In our factory, we almost had no communication with nearby villages. After all, there was a huge gap between them and us in many aspects, such as educational background, living habits, and our thoughts and way of thinking. Hence, we stayed with our colleagues every day and we knew each other very well. You know, love will come in time. So actually the problem of marriage was always solved internally. Ah, some beautiful women usually had many pursuers … In the 1980s, except for some demobilized soldiers who had already married before they came to the factory, the overwhelming majority of families had both members working in our factory.[10]

Mr. Ni's statement is not far from the truth. Among all the interviewees, only three had spouses who were not working in Jinjiang Factory. One was a housewife staying at home and the other two were peasants living in villages miles away. The internal marriages further increased every individual's scope for social interaction in the factory; the workers made friends not only by playing together but also by getting acquainted with their spouses' friends. As explained by Parkinson (2013), formal organization plays a role in shaping one's social world.

> In this world, A meets B outside of her daily social interactions (e.g. family, friends, neighbors) because of the ideological and organizational ties that place them in each other's spheres for the first time. B becomes part of A's regular circle; perhaps they get to know each other's families and friends, establishing an entirely new set of social network ties.

In sum, the factory was a closed, self-reliant society in terms of both subsistence and finding a partner. Due to its isolation, workers at Jinjiang Factory were firmly attached to their workplace in order to access daily entertainment, acquire social support, and restore day-to-day social relationships. In other words, workers of the Third Line Enterprises were highly dependent on their workplace. The organizational dependency has already been widely recognized as the main feature of Chinese urban SOEs and rural collectives. What, then, distinguishes the dependency of Third Line workers from that of the other two categories? This is the question that I now turn to.

3.6   URBAN FACTORIES, RURAL COLLECTIVES, AND THE THIRD LINE ENTERPRISES IN PERSPECTIVE

In the analysis of state and society relations in communist China, scholars have identified two distinctive social organizations exercising control over different sectors of Chinese society: factories in urban areas and collectives in rural ones. Strongly enforced workplace dependency is often conceived as one of the most influential elements that result in the state's domination over workers and peasants. As Andrew Walder notes, the workplace dependency could be comprehensively understood through two angles: what the actor could acquire from the workplace, on the one hand, and whether any alternatives existed, on the other (Walder 1986). Drawing on this explanation of dependency, this section shows that the Third Line enterprise differed from urban factories and rural collectives due to its unique location in an isolated mountain area. Deprived of other alternatives, workers in these factories exhibited a feature of "double dependency": they were dependent on the factory, first, for their economic, political, and social necessities and, second, for establishing and expanding their social relationships.

The organizational dependency of workers in urban factories is a result of the *danwei* (work unit) system. *Danwei*, generally speaking, is a general name for all the micro-organizations in communist China. In a city, a factory, a shop, a school, a hospital, a research institute, and a party organ, all can be called a *danwei* (Lu 1989). The *danwei* system is usually considered a social organizational system unique to China due to its substantial influence on an individual's everyday life. In addition to its function based on the division of labor in society—for a school to educate or a factory to manufacture—a work unit also plays a role in providing social services and protecting individuals against risks.[11] In communist China, workers received not only their wages and ration coupons for major consumer durables and daily necessities from their work units but also subsidies for food, staple goods, and residences. Moreover, the work unit also provided state labor insurance, welfare, and social security, and some social services such as medical care, daycare, and kindergarten for workers' children. Even so, the numerous material benefits are only one aspect of *danwei* functions. As Li Hanlin (1993, p. 23) argues, it took on an even wider range of political, judicial, civil, and social functions. As a result, it would be an exaggeration to assert that people in cities could survive without belonging to a work unit. In addition, the fact of workers' immobility within factories further enhanced their dependence on the work unit; with the very rare exceptions of skilled workers and people who had good relationships with leaders, the large majority of workers could not expect to transfer from one factory to another (Lu 1989, p. 77). In a word, a worker was tied to his/her work unit for life.

Virtually all China specialists agree that since the implementation of the *danwei* system, workers in urban areas were in fact living in a relatively isolated place and highly dependent on their workplace (Li et al. 1994; Liu 2002). Bray (2005, p. 200) even asserts, from a spatial perspective, that "each *danwei* became a financially independent economic unit with very little structural relationship to the rest of the city space that surrounded it. The wall enclosing the *danwei* simply reinforced, through symbolic representation, the actuality of this independence." Indeed, the isolation of a work unit and the dependency of a worker are quite clear when seen from the party leader's blueprint. Yet, it is much less so when we evaluate the degree of isolation and dependency based on the real everyday life of ordinary workers. As I have shown above, previous studies often illustrate the extent of workers' dependency by listing various necessities distributed by their workplace. All of these works take on a common perspective by focusing on the material provision of the work unit. Since this provision is not available to outsiders, it has been assumed in the literature that the more necessities a factory provides, the more dependent its workers will be. While the material provision of the work unit did shape workers' dependency in one respect, the resultant level of dependency is nevertheless the net effect of both the work unit's material supply and the workers' demands of their workplace. Due to the existence of alternatives, the two vectors do not move in the same direction.

One can broadly identify three categories of benefit conferred by the work unit: direct economic benefits, social services, and social relations. Workers might be able to find substitutes for the second and third of these in the city. Taking medical care as an example, even though it was commonly provided in every factory, workers—especially those in small and medium-sized ones—were more likely to seek medical services in public hospitals because the hospitals at their factories were usually small. In fact, they would more appropriately be called "clinics" than hospitals because the medical services provided were limited and extremely rudimentary.

The establishment of social relationships is another aspect in which workers might not necessarily be dependent on their work units. An obvious reason is the workers' freedom in finding a spouse. Indeed, some scholars have argued that intervention in workers' marriage and divorce was one of the multi-functions of the *danwei*. This was a formal power of the work unit, written on paper. However, the real impact of power on a person's life is determined not by whether it is written down but by the extent to which the power-holder is able to and wishes to use it. As a common Chinese saying goes, "Better to destroy ten temples than to destroy one marriage" (*ningchai shizuo miao, buhui yizhuang hun*); no leader was willing to damage a marriage as long as the bride and groom had acceptable political backgrounds. As a result, it was very common for a worker in one factory to find his or her spouse in other factories. Similarly, within a factory's living quarters, workers did not only come from one work unit.

Married urban workers, then, were subject to the influence of at least two work units: their own workplace and the one to which their spouses belonged. If their children were serving in a third factory, it made the problem even more complicated. Conventional wisdom has repeatedly emphasized the significance of living quarters and partially attributed workers' dependency and common identity to the independency of this spatial realm.[12] Unfortunately, the diversity of residents in the living quarters has been overlooked. This limitation is rooted in the stereotypical notion of social atomization and neglecting the role of family. Once family is taken into account, the work unit is no longer isolated from the rest of the city and becomes structurally embedded in the society that surrounds it.

Not only could the establishment of new social relationships go beyond the control of the unit but existing social relationships could also displace workers from their unit life. After all, "people's deep ties to their traditional seat of family and kinship had not been severed in a matter of decades" (Henderson and Cohen 1984, p. 139). Moreover, workers conceived friends with whom they had grown up or former classmates from school as more intimate companions than their current colleagues working in the same production line. Dittmer and Lü's (1996) study confirms this weak relationship with colleagues in the same unit. Through interviews conducted in Shanghai and Shijiazhuang, they found that the real friends to whom one could express one's innermost thoughts only existed outside the unit. Just as their informants said, "one should not mix *guanxi* [relationship, connection] with those you work with every day" (p. 257). Simply put, in terms of material provision, workers were highly dependent on their work units since they provided nearly all necessities. However, from the perspective of workers' demands in their everyday life—especially when taking into account the availability of alternatives in the city and their freedom in establishing social relationships—the workers' dependency on their workplace deserves a second thought. Henderson and Cohen (1984, p. 7–8) make a fair comment on the role of work unit in urban areas:

> The *danwei* system is, of course, not the sole force affecting the lives of work unit members. Other factors include the family, relationships with people outside the *danwei*, membership in neighborhood organizations, the power of the professional within a bureaucratic organization, constraints on middle-level leaders, and the influence of the communist party and other national organizations. Nevertheless, the *danwei* has an extraordinary influence on its individual members and (in our case) on the formal and informal relations among the hospital administrators, doctors, nurses, and patients.

This influence does not lessen the importance of the other factors, but rather interacts with them and provides an additional layer of control with which Chinese citizens must cope in their daily lives.

As for peasants' dependency on rural collectives, Vivienne Shue (1988) maintains that the rural politics of China had been dominated by a local particularism that predated the revolutionary. Even under Mao's communist regime, this pre-modern characteristic in rural China had never been destroyed. In a way, the people's commune movement launched in 1958 can be seen as an experiment in putting the rural populace under the control of the state. The spatial arrangement for mass mobilization is to collectively position the peasants in areas like the work units in cities. Lu (2003) indicates that, at the outset of the people's commune movement, many planners and architects were sent to the countryside and numerous fantasies about the new settlement were created. Due to the intertwined effects of natural calamities, policy deviation, the economic role of agriculture, and Soviet pressure for the repayment of debts, this utopian design eventually failed. As a result, the state's power had not been extended into the villages as far as was expected during the people's commune movement. It was, in fact, even further weakened by the decentralization of authority throughout the 1950s and 1960s. As Shue (1988, p. 55) argues, "by the mid-1960s ... the Chinese system of governance, planning, and administration had evolved into a curious amalgam in which decision-making authority was shared by center, region, and production unit". Local solidarity was also strengthened by the criss-crossed nature of Chinese administrative structures. Local cadres in this interlocking structure of horizontal and vertical units had to keep floating back and forth between the interest of their superiors and of their local constituents in order to successfully mobilize resources. Otherwise, they would sooner or later lose the game in a competitive system.

Since the state's power had never managed to destroy rural peripheral parochialism, the peasants were tightly bounded to their villages. This strong tie between peasants and villages was due to several things. First and foremost was the issue of subsistence. To use Oi's (1989, p. 1) language, it was the problem of "how the harvest shall be divided". In Mao's era, as Oi (1989, p. 7–10, 42) argues, even though the state attempted to dictate the division of the harvest through an elaborate set of regulations, such as the closing of grain markets, institutionalization of the unified purchase and supply, and the system of grain rationing, the state's authority was in fact dissolved by the patron–client relationship formed between the peasants and village cadres. In the Chinese rural periphery, therefore, the peasants' economic well-being was directly dependent on the corporate village. Oi's argument insinuates the relative autonomy of the rural periphery, but she does not extend this autonomy beyond the economic domain. In this respect, Vivienne Shue (1988, p. 49) offers a more comprehensive picture. Besides peasants' economic dependency, their social interactions also took on an inward-looking character. On the one hand, people usually gave priority to those in the same commune or the immediately neighboring one in their selection of marriage partners. In the 1970s, as noted by Shue (1988, p. 137), it was more and more common to match young people from the same brigade or village. On the other hand, however, peasants tended to make friends with those from their home commune as well. No matter how large the population was, the most meaningful social relationships for the peasants were only found within their own rural units. This important fact, together with three other integrations illustrated by Shue (1988, pp. 59–70)—political, economic, and normative—explained the strong tie between peasants and the communities they belonged to, which also differentiated the patterns of dependency between peasants and urban workers.[13] The cellular form of the rural units with high population density eventually gave rise to a honeycomb pattern in the social organizations of rural China (Shue 1988, p. 126–52).

The characteristics of urban workers' and peasants' patterns of dependency help us put the dependency of the Third Line workers in perspective. The dependency of the Third Line workers was similar to that of urban workers in that the enterprises were self-sufficient in providing direct material benefits and social services. But they differed in two fundamental respects. First, though most of the Third Line Enterprises had their own shuttle buses or even small trains to the nearest cities, the workers did not leave their factories except in special circumstances such as home leave or serious accidents. The factory sites were consequently the only place where workers and their children made a living. In their day-to-day life, the workers had no access to alternative social services or entertainment facilities beyond those in the factory. Second, and more importantly, in making friends or seeking their marriage partners, workers at Third Line Enterprises had no choice but their colleagues, due to the remoteness of their factory's location. This was especially the case for transferred workers. Unlike some demobilized soldiers and the Educated Youths whose homes were in nearby towns or villages, the transferred workers were almost completely cut off from their relatives and previous circles of friends. As a result, being stuck within those enclosed communities, they essentially had no opportunities to establish or expand their social relationships. In this sense, the dependency of Third Line workers was more like that of peasants in rural collectives. Nevertheless, in terms of the linkages to other surrounding communities, the Third Line Enterprises had a greater degree of discreteness because they were spread out and remotely situated, while the communes, brigades, and villages were contiguous to each other. Rather than the honeycomb pattern typical of rural collectives, the geographical distribution of Third Line Enterprises was jokingly described by the workers as "Goat Manure" to emphasize their separateness. The foregoing comparison among these three economic entities is summarized in Table 3.1.

As Table 3.1 shows, in terms of the angle of "what actors can acquire from the workplace", there seems to be no difference between urban SOEs, rural collectives, and Third Line Enterprises. However, if we compare them according to the second angle, "whether any alternatives exist", the differences are obvious. In essence, within the spectrum of members' dependency on their working communities, Third Line workers are at one extreme and urban factory workers at the other, with the peasants in rural collectives in between. The assertion that workers in Third Line Enterprises were living in the most isolated and independent situations is by no means imaginary, but a hard truth. Hidden in the mountains, these workers spent their lives in a limited space, sharing happiness and sadness with

Table 3.1 Comparison of the dependency in three economic entities

		Material benefits	Social services	Entertainment facilities	Social relations
Urban SOEs	Angle 1	√	√	√	√
	Angle 2	×	√	√	√
Rural Collectives	Angle 1	√	√	√	√
	Angle 2	×	×	×	√
Third Line	Angle 1	√	√	√	√
Enterprises	Angle 2	×	×	×	×

Notes: Material benefits refer to major consumer durables and daily necessities; social services include healthcare, education, and so on; entertainment facilities include museum, cinema, swimming pool, and so on; social relationships mainly refer to friendship and marriage. According to Andrew Walder (1986, pp. 14–5), Angle 1 refers to "what the actor can acquire from the workplace" and Angle 2 to "whether any alternatives exist" their immediate colleagues day after day. They were the workers who really embodied the slogan "Take the factory as home". In this respect, Jinjiang Factory is a good example. However, as discussed in Chapter 6, in contrast to the conventional wisdom that organizational dependency leads to the compliance of the Chinese working class, the higher degree of dependency in Jinjiang Factory did not give rise to a group of more obedient workers. Instead, the factory's production was constantly interrupted by the workers' absences.

3.7   Conclusion: City in the Village

The above account of Jinjiang Factory reveals that the Third Line Construction brought to life a number of remote, wild, and uncultivated spots in mountainous areas. In each of these newly created spots, a group of well-educated people were gathered and put in their efforts for the sake of industrial production. Transferred from leading cities, these people maintained their habits of urban life, which was in sharp contrast to the surrounding rural areas. With the development of the factory and the provision of essential supporting facilities, these previously uncultivated spots gradually developed into many "mini-cities" independent from the surrounding villages. It was precisely this unique characteristic of isolation that carved the featured relationship of workers and their workplaces.

Admittedly, to say that workers at Jinjiang Factory lived in an isolated situation does not mean that they had no connection with the surrounding rural areas and nearby cities in an absolute sense. As discussed in the above sections, peasants frequently dropped by to sell their vegetables or fruit,[14] and workers also went to Chengdu city and the regularly convened local market in the nearby villages.[15] But these activities did not have much impact on the internal social structure of Jinjiang Factory because they always occurred in an occasional and fleeting way. As a result, it was precisely their lives within the factory that led Jinjiang Factory workers to develop their particular social structure.

The story of Jinjiang Factory shows that workers in Third Line Enterprises were highly dependent on their workplace. They relied on the factory not only for acquiring the basic economic, political, and social necessities but also for building the day-to-day social networks (friendship and marriage) through the multifarious daily entertainment activities and a series of reciprocal interactions. I do not deny the existence of social networks of this type in urban factories. However, I do want to emphasize that this phenomenon was quintessential to the Third Line Enterprises rather than urban SOEs, simply because workers in mountainous areas had no alternatives outside their factories. If isolation and the high degree of dependency were features of Jinjiang Factory, then how did they affect the group leaders' governance? This is the question I turn to in the following two chapters.

Notes

1. The "7-21" Workers' University was the product of Mao's instruction on the cultivation of technicians, delivered on July 21, 1968. In this instruction, Mao recognized the experience of cultivating technical know-how in the Shanghai Machine Tool Factory and emphasized the necessity of cultivating technicians from experienced workers and farmers in other factories. As a result, many factories established their own "7-21" Workers' University.
2. This method of building, called *Gandalei*, was popular throughout the 1960s and 1970s due to savings of wood and bricks.
3. Interview with Chen Youbai.
4. Interestingly, other Third Line Enterprises I visited all had basketball courts and they were all named "the Lighting Court".
5. Interview with Zhu Guiqin.
6. Interview with Ni Tongzheng.
7. Interview with Huang Limin.
8. Interview with Tan Yi.
9. Interview with Chen Youbai.
10. Interview with Ni Tongzheng.
11. Almost all the work on the Chinese *danwei* system mentions its multiple functions (Lü and Perry 1997; Li 1993; Walder 1986; Henderson and Cohen 1984).
12. See, for example, Bray (2005).
13. Donnithorne (1972) claimed that, like the communes in rural area, the factories in cities were also in a relatively independent situation with relative autonomy. According to her, this relative autonomy should be partly attributed to the state's self-reliance and self-sufficiency policy for urban factories.
14. According to some interviewees (Ni Tongzheng, Wang Zhongtang, Li Guixiang, Ye Xingjian), interestingly, meal tickets from the Jinjiang Factory could be used as a kind of hard currency in the nearby village because the meal served in the factory's dining hall was very good. Peasants sometimes arrived to sell their vegetables just to get a factory meal ticket.

15. Peasants in the periodic local market even composed a jingle to describe the strong purchasing power of workers at the Jinjiang Factory: "Workers of the gear factory just look here and there, workers of Zhonghe factory could buy onions and garlic, and workers of Jinjiang Factory could even buy chicken and eggs" (*chilunchang dongzhang xikan, zhonghechang maicong maisuan, Jinjiangchang maiji maidan*).

REFERENCES

Bray, David. 2005. *Social Space and Governance in Urban China*, Stanford: Stanford University Press.

Dittmer, Lowell and Xiaobo Lü. 1996 (March). Personal Politics in the Chinese Danwei under Reform, *Asian Survey*, 36 (3):246–267.

Donnithorne, Andrey. 1972 (October–December). China's Cellular Economy: Some Economic Trends Since the Cultural Revolution, *China Quarterly*, 52:605–612.

Gould, Roger V. 1995. *Insurgent Identities: Class, Community, and Protest in Paris from 1848 to the Commune*, Chicago: University of Chicago Press.

Henderson, Gail and Myron S. Cohen. 1984. *The Chinese Hospital: A Socialist Work Unit*, New Haven and London: Yale University Press.

Li, Hanlin. 1993. China's Danwei Phenomenon and the Mechanisms of Conformity in Urban Communities, *Sociology Research*, 5:23–32.

Li, Lulu, Hanlin Li and Fenyu Wang. 1994. China's Danwei Phenomenon and Structural Reform, *Chinese Social Sciences Quarterly*, 2: 5–16.

Liu, Jianjun. 2002. *The Danwei China: Individual, Organization and the State in the System of Social Control*, Tianjin: Tianjin People's Publishing House.

Lu, Feng. 1989. Danwei: A Unique Form of Social Organization, *Chinese Social Science*, 1:71–88.

Lu, Duanfang. 2003. *Building the Chinese Work Unit: Modernity, Scarcity and Space, 1949–2000*, PhD dissertation, University of California, Berkeley.

Lü, Xiaobo and Elizabeth J. Perry, eds. 1997. *Danwei: The Changing Chinese Workplace in Historical and Comparative Perspective*, Armonk, NY: M.E. Sharpe.

Oi, C. Jean. 1989. *State and Peasant in Contemporary China: The Political Economy of Village Government*, Berkeley and Los Angeles: University of California Press.

Parkinson, Sarah Elizabeth. 2013 (August). Organizing Rebellion: Rethinking High-Risk Mobilization and Social Networks in War. *American Political Science Review*, 107 (3):418–432.

Shue, Vivienne. 1988. *The Reach of the State: Sketches of the Chinese Body Politics*, Stanford: Stanford University Press.

The Committee of Chengdu Local Chronicles. 1995. *The Local Chronicles of Chengdu: The Chronicle of Machinery Industry*, Chengdu: Chengdu Publishing House.

The Office of Factory Chronicle. 1986. *Jinjiang Oil Pump and Oil Nozzle Factory, Factory Chronicle: 1966–1985*.

Walder, Andrew G. 1986. *Communist Neo-Traditionalism: Work and Authority in Chinese Industry*, Berkeley: University of California Press.

Yeh, Wen-hsin. 1997. Republican Origins of the Danwei: The Case of Shanghai's Bank of China, in Lü, Xiaobo and Elizabeth J. Perry, eds. *Danwei: The Changing Chinese Workplace in Historical and Comparative Perspective*, Armonk, NY: M.E. Sharpe, 60–88.

CHAPTER 4

The Context of Toleration (2): Interconnected Social Networks

This chapter reveals the emotional basis for the tolerating governance in the Jinjiang Factory: interconnected social networks. I will argue that the interconnected social networks complicated interpersonal relationships in the workshop. In particular, the formal relationships between workers and managers were intertwined with informal ones such as friends, relatives, or even husband and wife. Over time, the boundary between the family and the factory was blurred. In such circumstances, the group leaders had less incentive to reinforce the formal rules strictly. In the following sections, I first introduce the three groups of workers in Jinjiang Factory. I then show how these groups were fixed in the workshop and how they perceived each other in their day-to-day interaction. In the fourth section, I illustrate how these fragmentations produced the interconnected social networks in Jinjiang Factory. The fifth section distinguishes the interconnected social networks in Third Line Enterprises from that in urban SOEs. The sixth section concludes this chapter.

4.1 THREE GROUPS OF WORKERS

There were three groups of people among the workers at Jinjiang Factory. Each group was identified by a common name indicating its workers' similarities in training, salary, educational background, and skill level. The three names (labels) were transferred workers (*zhinei zhigong*), Returned Educated Youth (*fancheng zhiqing*), and demobilized soldiers (*fuyuan junren*)

© The Author(s) 2018
C. Chen, *Toleration*, New Perspectives on Chinese Politics and Society, https://doi.org/10.1007/978-981-10-8941-1_4

"Transferred workers" were workers from the coastal provinces in the East. In the early days of Jinjiang Factory (1970–1973), hundreds of workers in Tianjin, Shanghai, Wuxi, Hangzhou, and Luoyang were transferred to the factory and formed the majority of its labor force. Among these transferred workers of diverse origins, natives of Shanghai overwhelmingly outnumbered workers from other places simply because the factory was built to a contract with the Shanghai Diesel Engine Factory. By the end of the early 1980s, 659 of the total 840 transferred workers came from Shanghai. It is noteworthy that there were also divisions among the transferred workers in respect of the salary policies applied to them. Taking Shanghai workers, the largest group of transferred workers, as an example, 429 workers were previously employed by the Shanghai Diesel Engine Factory or Shanghai Construction Mechanical Engineering Factory, while the other 230 were not formally employed but worked as interns or apprentices. As a result, the former group could be paid according to the standard of Shanghai (though their residence registration, *Hukou*, was also transferred to Chengdu), while the latter group had to be paid according to the local Sichuan standard, which was usually 3–5 yuan per month less. Since these 230 workers all graduated from the technical school of the Shanghai Diesel Engine Factory, people gave them another label, as *Jixiaosheng* ("students of the technical school").

In the mid- and late 1970s, the recruitment of Returned Educated Youth further diversified the labor profile of Jinjiang Factory. As Gold and McLaren described, in the late 1970s, thousands of Educated Youths who had been sent to the countryside were repatriated to their home city of Shanghai (Gold 1980; McLaren 1979). However, the widespread unemployment of these Returned Educated Youths immediately became one of Shanghai's biggest problems. In the nationwide "Current of Returning to the City", the problem of unemployment of the returned youths in Chengdu was no less serious than that in Shanghai. Jinjiang Factory, as one of the 30 provincial large-scale Enterprises, was one of the major employers of these Returned Educated Youths (Sichuan Provincial Department of Machinery Industry 1985). In the late 1970s, Jinjiang Factory continuously hired about 900 Returned Educated Youths in total, which constituted almost one-third of the factory's workers at the time. Before being formally employed as a permanent worker, all these Returned Educated Youths were assigned for three years as apprentices to the "Construction Team" (*jijiandui*) and they were paid 17.5 yuan per month. At the end of the apprenticeship, if shown by testing to be qualified, they would become permanent workers at the factory and start work in the first grade (*yiji gong*).[1] At that time, their salary would be increased to 21.5 yuan. In this respect, the transferred workers were much better off. Even the *Jixiaosheng* did not need to undergo the three years of apprenticeship in the newly established factory and could be directly placed in the second grade (*erji gong*), with a monthly salary of 31.5 yuan.

The demobilized soldiers, who were usually considered highly politically credible, constituted the third group of Jinjiang Factory's labor force. Admittedly, the recruitment of demobilized soldiers was not unique to Third Line Enterprises. Perry notes that demobilized peasant soldiers accounted for a large proportion of workers in Chinese SOEs (Perry 1994). Nevertheless, few urban Enterprises had as many demobilized soldiers as Jinjiang Factory, where they could even act as an independently influential group. After all, urban Enterprises had to absorb the numerous laborers who were city dwellers first. Throughout the 1980s and 1990s, more than one-sixth of the workers at Jinjiang Factory were demobilized soldiers from nearby villages. Compared to the transferred workers and the Returned Educated Youths, who at least had finished high school, these demobilized soldiers were mostly illiterate peasants. However, their poor educational background did not restrict their entitlement to privileges. Like their colleagues the *Jixiaosheng*, they could skip the apprenticeship stage and enjoy the pay of first-grade workers. Even though they were paid 10 yuan per month less than the *Jixiaosheng*, their access to land somewhat alleviated their burden in raising a family. Some would even give up their extra award and save more of their time to take care of their crops, as the following conversation illustrates:

> "To be honest, I did not care about the extra award. For those at most 5 to 10 yuan, I had to exhaust myself every day. Then who would take care of my land in the village? I need to ride for two hours to the land by bicycle!"
>
> "Why did not you hire someone?" I asked.
>
> "How could I afford that? Besides, the person I hired might not be better than me. It was not worthwhile to sacrifice my harvest just for a few yuan!"[2]

In a word, due to their different backgrounds, workers in each group had a different name indicating the shared origins and features associated with it. When someone was mentioned as a transferred worker, it usually implied a skilled, well-educated person living an urban life style; if categorized as Returned Educated Youth, he/she was usually considered educated but unskilled. The term "demobilized soldiers" had a variant in the factory, *laozhuan* ("the elder demobilized"), a somewhat belittling name usually referring to the most illiterate and unskilled segment of the labor force.

There are exceptions to these generalizations, of course. For example, my interviewee Ye Xingjian was one of the Educated Youth workers. Through assiduous work and study in the Machinery Workshop as an ordinary worker, he not only outperformed many transferred skilled workers in practical operations but also published several journal articles dealing with difficult technical problems. Since Jinjiang Factory's bankruptcy, he has been hired by a university in Chengdu as a lecturer. Ye Xingjian is not the only one who does not fit in the abovementioned broad categories. On the whole, however, some common features could be identified for the majority of workers in each group.

4.2   GROUP BELONGING AND JOB OPPORTUNITY IN JINJIANG FACTORY

In her analysis of workers' fragmentation in Shanghai, Perry showed that the workers' occupational opportunity was intimately associated with their place of origin (Perry 1993). Interestingly, a similar phenomenon also occurred in Jinjiang Factory in that workers from the same group congregated in a particular job niche in the factory. Occupational segmentation by groups thus further fostered and solidified the separation of workers. How, then, were workers' groups in Jinjiang Factory associated with different job niches? To answer this question, it is necessary first to clarify the concepts of "the front" and "the rear", a general categorization of occupational opportunities in the factory coined by the workers themselves.

The terms "the front" (*qianfang*) and "the rear" (*houfang*) were actually borrowed from their usage in warfare, referring to the front (battlefield) and the rear (support), respectively. Hence, "the front" of the factory generally included those departments, workshops, and offices which took part in the production process, while "the rear" referred to those sections providing support services. It is noteworthy that this bifurcation was made by workers at different levels of the factory's hierarchy. At the highest level, the division existed between the workshops and the factory management departments as well as other logistics sections, such as the team of trucks (*chedui*). At the intermediate level, "the front" and "the rear" categorized different workshops. The Machinery, Matching Parts, Heat Treatment, Casting and Forging, and Preparation workshops were all *front* workshops involved in production, while the Instrument Production Workshop and the Machine Fixing Workshop were regarded as the rear ones. The Division between the "front" and the "rear" could also be found in each workshop, at the lowest level. For example, the Matching Parts Workshop had the most workers of any workshop at Jinjiang Factory. Every worker in it belonged to one of five groups: planning, technology, production, washing, and assisting. The production group, which accounted for 295 of the 393 workers in the workshop, was the only group not categorized as "rear" (Jinjiang Oil Pump and Nozzle Factory 1983).

The occupational opportunities in "the front" and "the rear" at different levels were filled with workers from particular groups. Since the late 1970s and early 1980s, a general pattern of occupational segmentation among workers had gradually appeared in the factory: the transferred workers accounted for the majority in the rear sections, while the demobilized workers and Returned Educated Youths made up most of the labor force in the front. Specifically, through the 1980s and the early 1990s, the transferred workers, especially those from Shanghai, mostly worked in the factory's management. Those who failed to become members of the factory staff usually transferred between or within workshops from the front to the rear. Two things might explain such a pattern. First, compared to the Returned Educated Youths and demobilized soldiers, the transferred workers were on average more senior, more skillful, and more experienced, and it therefore seemed more proper to let them take charge of the work on planning, managing, supervision, and so on. Second, since the Retuned Educated Youths and most of the demobilized soldiers were younger than the transferred workers, it was reasonable to let them shoulder the burden of heavy work in the front positions. As a result, the Returned Educated Youths and demobilized soldiers constituted the overwhelming majority of the labor force in the front job slots of the front workshops. But again, the distinction in practice was not as neat and stark as this. Typical outliers were the demobilized soldiers who had previously held positions above Platoon Leader. These former military officers usually assumed the position of Party Branch Secretary in the factory workshops. This group was, however, small in number, and not big enough to change the association of workers' occupational opportunities with their group belongings in general.

Conventional wisdom has repeatedly emphasized the role of gender in weakening the labor force as a whole (Glickman 1984; Tilly 1986; Perry 1993). Jinjiang Factory was no exception, as the gender variable indeed affected the differentiation of workers' jobs in the factory. After the Matching Parts Workshop (393 workers), the Machinery Workshop was the second biggest in the factory, with 246 workers. The production of these two workshops was in stark contrast to their skills requirements. The task of the Matching Parts Workshop was to accurately match the nozzle needle with the needle housing, to a level of precision of microns, while the work in the Machinery Workshop, on the other hand, mainly consisted of grinding, fitting, lathing, and so on. The former task thus required extreme patience and care, while the latter needed sufficient physical strength to operate and lift perhaps the heaviest machinery and units in the factory. Female workers therefore became the majority in the skilled workshop, while male workers dominated the relatively less-skilled ones. This was in contrast to the pattern described by some previous studies.[3] The difference between these two workshops can be better understood from Fig. 4.1. It can be seen that the machines in the Matching Parts Workshop were much smaller than those in the Machinery Workshop. With these small machines, however, workers could not perform their jobs without light from lamps even in daylight, which hinted at the degree of precision and difficulty in their job. As a result, "more than 60% of workers in my workshop (the Matching Parts Workshop) were female workers".[4]

Over time, segmentation according to group belongings became more established by the nature of the workers' job assignments. The transferred workers sat in the rear as managers, production planners, quota setters, technology supervisors, timers, and so on, while the Returned Educated Youths and demobilized soldiers were on their feet in the front and shouldered the majority of the production work. Gender also played an important role in determining workers' assignment to workshops. It further divided the front workers and gave different workshops unique recruitment preferences. If labels, as well as occupational niches in the factory, have well-delineated distinctions among workers, in what way did they affect the relationship, friendly or unfriendly, among workers? After all, the group belonging and occupational positions per se have played no part at this point. To answer this question, we need to go beyond abstract theoretical inference and focus on the specific and clear

Fig. 4.1 The Matching Parts and Machinery Workshops. (Above: workers in the Matching Parts Workshop. Below: a section (*gongduan*) of the Machinery Workshop)

day-to-day activities of workers. In the next two sections, I argue that, through the workers' day-to-day interactions outside the workshops as well as the activities inside them, group belongings were transformed from abstract names to real practices. Different labels signified differences not only in appearance, such as clothing styles and hobbies, but also in mutual perceptions and attitudes.

4.3   Fragmentation in Daily Lives

Life Outside the Workshop

Differences can be observed and seen to expand in the details of workers' daily life. By studying women workers in cotton mills in Shanghai, Emily Honing found that dress style, eating habits, marriage customs, and dialects constituted the basis of the most important divisions and antagonisms among workers (Honing 1986, p. 5). Perry (1993, p. 59) also observed similar phenomena among the women cotton workers in the Jiangnan and Subei areas. In Jinjiang Factory, these details of workers' daily lives played the same role in shaping the mutual impressions of workers.

Dacron (transliterated to Chinese as *diqueliang*) may be the most popular fabric in the 1970s and the 1980s. It was imported from overseas and first sold in Guangzhou, before quickly becoming a precious fabric in the cities of eastern provinces. Due to its scarcity in the market, clothes made of Dacron were usually much more expensive than cotton ones. At the time, owning a Dacron shirt could even be regarded as a symbol of high status. Dacron clothes were rarely seen in the local stores of Chengdu, however, let alone the Supply and Marketing Cooperative (*gongxiaoshe*) in the villages. The high price also prevented the Returned Educated Youths and demobilized soldiers from buying their much-desired Dacron clothes. As a worker recalled, in the 1970s, a Dacron shirt would cost no less than 5 yuan with clothing coupon, while his basic salary was a mere 21.5 yuan. In the factory, therefore, workers who were Returned Educated Youths and demobilized soldiers usually wore clothes made of coarse materials in subdued colors. The attire among transferred workers, especially those from Shanghai, was much smarter. Many of them possessed Dacron clothes in bright colors, which were easily recognized by others in the factory. One of my informants, a transferred worker from Shanghai, explicitly expressed her pride in her dress:

> We had shirts made of Dacron! Those local workers were not able to buy them and they envied us very much. When you were walking in the factory, you could even identify the transferred workers from others merely by their clothing. In the late 1980s, as they [Returned Educated Youth, demobilized soldiers, and some other local workers] got richer and richer, they always entrusted us to buy these smart clothes from Shanghai. So every time I came back from my home leave in Shanghai, I took several large packages with

me, full of all the stuff they wanted. The most popular items were leather shoes and shirts of new designs.[5]

Dacron clothes were quite novel for local workers, but they were by no means the only thing brought by the transferred workers that attracted the attentions of their local colleagues. Many transferred workers also moved their furniture, beds, shelves, wardrobes, and even coal stoves, from the eastern cities to the mountain area. Each of those new-fashioned designs always gave rise to a surge of imitation. A typical example was the popularity of the design called "Tiger Claw" (*laohu jiao*). This was originally a design for the legs of wardrobes used by Shanghai workers. Local workers later imitated this design and applied it to their tables, beds, and other pieces of furniture. As one informant recalled as she guided me to her room and pointed at the wardrobe:

> Do not look down upon this wardrobe. You could only apply for one at the time you registered [your] marriage. When we moved it here from Shanghai, the local workers were amazed by its design. … (She bent down) … Look at this. It was called Tiger Claw and many locals once came to look at it and measure it. Soon after, it became one of the most popular designs for local furniture. But their imitation was never as beautiful as ours from Shanghai.[6]

Thanks to their unbroken links with the eastern cities, the transferred workers could enjoy access to many daily necessities not available to local workers. In order to ensure the continual provision of these, the transferred workers had to use all possible opportunities to go back to their home cities and took as much as possible of these items each time:

> Many things we needed were not available here. Some of them could not even easily be found in Chengdu. Soap, sugar and the type of dried noodle which was my son's favorite, for example, were all brought in from Shanghai. That was why I had to go back, even though the train ticket was very expensive. In 1976, the ticket for a hard-cushioned train from Chengdu to Shanghai was 34.2 yuan; the hard berth was 58 yuan, while my salary was only 31.5 yuan per month. Basically, I went every 18 months and, every time I came back, my hands were full of bags. We always laughingly said that our salaries all contributed to the construction of our nation's railways.[7]

The differences between workers could also be observed through their daily recreational activities. Generally speaking, board games, physical exercise, and artistic and cultural activities were the most popular in the factory. Among these, most transferred workers would choose to be involved in artistic and cultural activities, such as practicing calligraphy, playing musical instruments, reading books, writing poems, and carving seals, while the Returned Educated Youth workers preferred to play board games, of which Chinese chess, bridge, and mahjong were the most popular. Some of the peasant demobilized soldiers had to do their farm work after their work in the factory, while the others were more likely to join the Returned Educated Youth workers for board games. Sports and physical exercise appeared to be the common interest of the three groups of workers, but the players would usually partner with workers from the same group. The different hobbies among workers were clearly identified by one informant:

> People from this region [Sichuan Province] liked playing mahjong and cards very much. Those Educated Youth workers and some of the demobilized soldiers even arranged to meet up during working hours in the workshop. They invited their mahjong and cards partners and discussed whose home they would go to after dinner. They knew how to enjoy their lives. We transferred workers did not like playing mahjong. In our spare time, we usually played badminton, read books or newspapers, wrote diaries and some essays, drew pictures or did seal carving.[8]

This informant's observation could be corroborated by some common patterns among workers in Jinjiang Factory. All the transferred workers interviewed reported reading books and playing ball games as their most preferred pastimes, while more than 80% of the Returned Educated Youth and demobilized soldiers reported chess and various card games as their favorite leisure activities.[9] Pierre Bourdieu (1991) once argued that the probabilities of practicing different sports (used as a general term) were contingent on one's economic capital, cultural capital, spare time, and family tradition as well as early training; the distribution of hobbies among workers at Jinjiang Factory revealed their distinguishing characteristics along these lines, which delineated the boundaries between one group and another.

Clothes, daily necessities, furniture, and hobbies were indeed minor details of life, but as a form of culture in the factory they became outward manifestations of different labels, distinguishing one group of workers from another. Moreover, this culture gave rise to a public image of those transferred workers as fashion-conscious, well-educated people with cosmopolitan tastes, which further enhanced their sense of superiority and strengthened their self-identification of the label "transferred workers": they were missionaries from the country's most developed region coming to Chengdu to evangelize.

Life in the Workshop

Workshops were another crucial site shaping workers' perceptions toward others. In the production process, workers' interactions characterized their relationships, competition, or cooperation in a particular way.[10] Frequent frictions due to differences in working skills, seniority, and working attitude made the division among workers visible and relevant to all. It was through day-to-day interactions in the workshop that the label of each group was bestowed with meanings beyond a common name or identity, which in turn shaped the workers' impressions and attitudes toward each other and ultimately affected their mutual relationships.

Whenever the production task in the "front" workshops was intensive, the factory mobilized workers in the rear to provide help. This policy was supposed to be a win-win game for both camps of workers. On one hand, workers in the rear could get some extra pay; on the other hand, the workload of workers in the front could be reduced. However, instead of strengthening the worker's solidarity, the support provided by "the rear" workshop (mainly made up of transferred workers) to "the front" ones (mainly Returned Educated Youths and demobilized soldiers) turned out to have exacerbated the division among workers.

Why did a supposedly mutually beneficial arrangement lead to greater fragmentation? The key was that the temporarily relocated workers in the front workshops were motivated by financial and reputational incentives and tended to exceed their production quota. The excess bonus might be the most straightforward and effective of the various incentives because, for many workers in the rear shops, this bonus was very hard to obtain.

As mentioned above, the rear workshops were not directly involved in manufacturing, but offered various forms of assistance to the front workshops so as to make production smoother and more efficient. The nature of the work in the rear workshops was therefore different from that in the front ones. Let us take the Instrument Production Workshop and the Machinery Workshop as examples for comparison. Workers in the former mainly worked on the production of special tools needed for some specific processing procedure but which could not be found in the market. Cutters were one type of such tools required for component processing. Besides some normal cutting, the multifarious design of the components required distinctive cutting work to be performed with uniquely designed cutters. These unconventionally shaped cutters were the "products" of the Instrument Production Workshop. Usually, as each particular instrument was only required by one workshop, one section, or sometimes even one production group, the total number of such products required was no more than a few dozens, sometimes even fewer than ten. In stark contrast, workers in the Machinery Workshop had a much heavier workload. They took charge of the basic processing job, such as cutting, grinding, fitting, and lathing. Even though they did not have to be bothered by making tools in strange shapes, they were required to fulfill their monthly production quota. The Instrument Production Workshop and the Machinery Workshop could therefore be classified as "technology intensive" and "labor intensive" respectively. In other words, workers in the rear shops such as Workshop of Instrument Production Workshop were doing technologically complicated but small-scale work. It was therefore very common for the workers in this shop to have almost completed the required number of their "products" (e.g. special tools) shortly after they became proficient at their production. Exceeding the quota was therefore out of the question. In contrast, jobs in the front shops were technologically simple but quantitatively large and were undoubtedly easier for workers to increase their income by receiving the excess bonus. This was especially the case for the workers called up from the rear, who were more skilled than those in the front.

Besides the formally established material incentives, some informal cultural factors, such as the concern about *mianzi* ("face") and personal dignity, also played a role in motivating the temporarily located workers to exceed their quota. Workers in the rear shops were mainly transferred workers, who were supposed to be more experienced and skilled than the Returned Educated Youths and demobilized soldiers. When they were moved from the rear to the front, if they had failed to do their work better than others in terms of quantity and quality, they would have felt shamed and worried about being mocked by their colleagues. Zhu Guiqin described her experience of supporting workers in the Machinery Workshop:

> When the production task was heavy, the factory always mobilized the workers in the rear to give support to the front. When we were moved to the

front shops, we usually worked very hard. But many people just wanted to show off and tried very hard to outperform others. Actually, this kind of act was very likely to create resentment among workers in the front shops. I did not do this ... Every time I finished my quota, I would stop and wait for others. Once, a young worker came to me after work and said, "Zhu *shifu* (Fellow Zhu), you did it so fast!" I replied "Actually, I could even save another one and half hours!" Even though I would not exceed them in production, I think I needed to tell them the truth and let them see the gap between them and us. After all, most of us workers from the rear shops were more experienced, more senior, and more skilled than them. If our working speed could not exceed theirs, we would lose face and they would mock us behind our backs.[11]

As Zhu mentioned, workers in the front shop were not grateful for the support of the workers from the rear. On the contrary, they were more likely to be irritated by their hard work and blame the helping workers. It was not because the moved workers took the bonus that should have had belonged to them. No matter how much extra money the moved workers earned during the month(s) in the front shops, they were working on a temporary basis and would sooner or later go back to their original work-shops. In fact, what worried the front workers a lot was that their production quota was very likely to be increased in future due to the hard work of the rear workers. In every workshop, the quota setters (*ding e yuan*) adjusted the quota of each procedure and each component every month according to the workers' monthly performance. If many of the moved workers were able to complete the same production quota in a much shorter time, the quota setters would think that the existing quota in fact underestimated the workers' productiveness. Surely, large quota adjustments could not be made casually and easily, but the working records of the moved workers would certainly be an important benchmark for future quota increases. Moreover, the production quota was also rigid in nature and, once increased, would never fall back. In other words, the hard work of the moved workers could have a permanent effect on the workload of the workers in the front shops. When I asked my informant Zhu Guiqin why she did not exceed the production quota as others did, she answered:

Some shifted workers' hard work could possibly increase the production quota of the whole section they were in. It was not a big deal for us shifted workers because we only worked there for a while, but the front workers had to work there for their whole life![12]

In a word, in the process of supporting the front workshops, the horizontal division among workers was entrenched. On the one hand, the moved rear workers were motivated, formally and informally, to exceed their production quota; on the other hand, the front workers were very likely to be burdened in the future with higher production targets. On the surface, this seemed to be a division between the rear and the front workshops. Looking deeper, however, it was in fact a division between workers with different labels. Ironically, though some transferred workers indeed appeared more considerate than others, like the informant Zhu Guiqin, their explicit claims of superior skills and strong desire to distinguish themselves from others achieved an effect no less than their colleagues in separating themselves from the front workers.

It is worth noting that the tension between the front and rear workers discussed here is different from that between the temporary and permanent workers discussed earlier (Perry 1994; Lin 2009). According to Blecher (1984), temporary contract workers are "peasants who have been hired by urban state/collective sector industrial Enterprises through contracts with their rural collectives. Although temporary contract work is often not very temporary at all … the contract workers retain the official status of rural householders, and maintain their permanent home in their villages." The tension between front and rear workers is therefore different from that between the temporary and permanent workers in at least two respects. First, the former occurs among all permanent workers, while the latter occurs between workers of different employment status. Second, the former happens intrinsically because of the discrimination of one group of workers against another, while the latter is a consequence of discriminatory state policies. As a result, the former is more likely to worsen the relationship among workers than the latter.

The sense of skills superiority also gave rise to a discriminatory attitude by the transferred workers toward their local colleagues. The worst victims might be the demobilized soldiers. In Jinjiang Factory, the transferred workers gave them a new group name, *laozhuan* ("the elder demobilized"). The demobilized soldiers were, on average, actually no older than the transferred workers; on the contrary, they were in fact much younger. The name *laozhuan* was used to express the transferred workers' dislike and belittlement of the demobilized soldiers' illiteracy, lack of skills, and nonchalant working attitudes. The informant Liu Chengmin complained that:

> Those demobilized soldiers and some Returned Educated Youths were illiterate and unskilled. Most importantly, I think they had the peasant mentality,

that is, they were calculating and unwilling to make even the smallest sacrifice. Also, they did not do their work carefully and seriously. In the foundry, when we were making the models, any foreign substance was not acceptable. But many of those workers in the shop were not as responsible as us. Several times, I clearly saw some sand in the mold, but they still poured the molten iron into it. I tried to stop them and asked them to clean the mold first. But they just ignored me.[13]

It goes without saying that there were many demobilized soldiers who worked carefully, and some were even technologically outstanding. However, the discriminatory perceptions held by the transferred workers toward the demobilized soldiers were pretty stubborn once they were labeled *laozhuan*. As the informant LanQingshan recalled,

Those transferred workers and *Jixiaosheng* always looked down on me. I started my work in this factory under the tutelage of a Shanghai master worker. On the first day he instructed me, he said to me "When you finish your study with me, as long as there is no one laughing at you behind your back, you should be satisfied." To be honest, that really struck me. Since then, when others completed their work and went to play elsewhere, I stayed on to read the learning materials. I would not leave even when they invited me to play with them. I actually became quite skillful in two years. Once there was a test for the skill of grinding, and 200 workers in total registered for the test. The workshop director asked me "What ranking do you expect?" I answered "Maybe the top six." The director laughed and said, "Top six? Don't even think about it!" At that time, there was also another Shanghai worker standing beside the director. He sneered and pointed his little finger at me. Seeing their reactions, I changed my goal immediately and said, "I will be in the top three". When the test had finished, the director asked how I had done. I told him I got 90-plus in the theoretical test, and thought I could score full marks in the practical test. He questioned this and said, "Impossible, no one can get full marks!" Then he ran to the lathe I operated and carefully checked my work. After checking for a while, he claimed that I had not cleaned the machine very well after using it and deducted two points. So in the end, I got 98.[14]

This was not the first time that LanQingshan experienced discrimination and unfortunately it was not the last time either:

The factory frequently held skills examinations. Once, a Shanghai worker asked me "Do you want to get the awards for this examination?" I asked, "How much is the first prize?" "30 yuan", he said. "OK, then I want to come top." He laughed and said, "Are you kidding? You think you can be the first, with your poor skills?" I felt offended and responded, "If I am not in the top three, I will give up my basic wage. Or your workshop can treat me to a meal – deal?" When I knew I was the top scorer in the examination, I went to his workshop and asked him to deliver on his promise. The director gave me another 30 yuan and asked me to buy the meal myself. They were very smart and knew they had to spend a lot more on treating me because I was certain to invite dozens of my friends to enjoy the meal with me![15]

After LanQingshan completed his studies with the master worker, he worked independently in the Instrument Production Workshop. But the misery did not end with his appointment in the factory's "technology intensive" section:

Once they asked me to make an eccentric cutter (*pianxin daopai*). As I saw the design drawing, I found some mistakes in the basic technical specifications. I told the designer, a Shanghai master worker, but he ignored my suggestions and just asked me to do it strictly according to his design. I declined, and asked him who would be responsible if in the end all the cutters turned out to be useless. He said he would take the responsibility. But I think he could not afford it, because it would be a great waste of materials. Even worse, it might slow down the pace of production in the front workshops. Then he turned to someone else for help. They made eight in total, and seven of them were discarded because they could not be used. That designer came to me again and tried to persuade me to make it. I told him I could not do it unless he followed my suggestion and revised those wrong specifications. I did it for him till 11 pm and only one out of the eight failed.[16]

Fellow Li (*Li shifu*) was a fitter at the factory. Once he needed me to process a component for him. He told me the basic technical details orally. I tried three times and they all failed. Then I approached him and asked him if there might be a problem with his technical data. He insisted that his data was correct and said scornfully, "What the hell would you know about it?" I was so annoyed and refused to do it anymore. He did the work himself many times and all of them failed. He was so angry that he forcefully smashed a useless one onto the floor. Finally, he invited the workshop director to negotiate with me and wanted me to offer help. At the time, I was still angry and said to him satirically, "Just smash the lathe machine, if you dare! You are a *Jixiaosheng*. But I am afraid you cannot even read the caliper!"[17]

It must be said that LanQingshan's unhappy encounters were probably extreme examples because people were more likely to keep their negative attitudes toward others to themselves rather than making them explicit. However, these unspoken perceptions and attitudes would not disappear just because of efforts to hide them. It was an insidious source of fragmentation deep in the minds of the workers, strengthening the intra-group recognition and diminishing the prospect of inter-group solidarity in the process. Once a trigger appeared, such as the quarrel that LanQingshan encountered, the concealed disharmony among workers of different labels was exposed in public.

Wage increases are a typical trigger of that effect. From 1963 to 1977, Chinese workers' wages were virtually unchanged in numerical terms and workers entering the labor force during this period received the lowest levels of pay (Walder 1987). Although workers in Third Line Enterprises were paid a little more than others due to the policy privilege, their wages had also been frozen since their recruitment in the late 1960s and early 1970s. It was not until the end of the Cultural Revolution that workers finally had their wages increased for the first time. Throughout the late 1970s and 1980s, Jinjiang Factory initiated four wage increases in total, in 1979, 1983, 1985, and 1987. None of the increases, however, covered all employees at the factory. Each time only 40% of the staff was entitled to the salary increase. The factory usually set the level for each department (various administrative departments, workshops, the factory hospital, and the factory-affiliated schools were all included) in proportion to its share of total employment and devolved the power of selection down to the lower organizations. In the course of competing for selection, workers immediately split up when making their claims in order to become one of the beneficiaries. As Tan Yi, who was the Party Branch Secretary in the Heat Treatment Workshop, recalled:

> In the Working Conference on Wage Increase, the representatives started quarrelling with each other very easily. The demobilized soldiers claimed based on their laborious work in the front; the transferred workers claimed for their seniority. As for the Returned Educated Youth workers, according to the national policy, the period for which they went to the countryside and became members of production teams was also counted toward their length of service. Accordingly, even though they entered the factory some years later, they were not considered less senior than others and, based on that, they also claimed their wage increases.[18]

As the interviewee informed me, similar phenomena could also be observed in the Matching Parts, Machinery, and Instrument Production workshops.[19] In order to avoid conflicts among workers, many of these sub-organizations drew up their selection list by secret ballot. Unfortunately, this did not ameliorate the fragmentation of workers as expected, due to the prevalent practice of private canvassing. Ni Tongzheng recalled his experience working in Jinjiang Factory Technical School:

> "It was around 1982 or 1983 when we had the chance of a wage increase. The wage increase could only cover 40% of us, but for someone who had made great contributions to the factory, his/her wage could be increased by two grades. At that time, besides my job in the factory technical school, I also worked as the director of the internship workshop (*shixi chejian*). Actually I did a lot more. For example, I did a lot of secretarial work for the school principal and helped to promote cooperation between factory workshops and external organizations. Given all that I did for the school and factory, the school principal, vice-principal and even the Party Branch Secretary, they all wanted to increase my wage by two grades."
>
> "Where did they come from?" I asked. "Were they all from Shanghai, like you?"
>
> "Yes, they were all from Shanghai. At the time, I was competing with a demobilized soldier, who was much older than me and was in charge of ideological and political work in the school. To be honest, he worked very conscientiously, but his position in the school belonged to the rear section, which was considered unimportant. In order to make sure I could have my wage increased by two grades successfully, we did a lot of work in private. All those leaders who supported me helped me to win the votes. They persuaded all the other teachers and staff workers who came from Shanghai to vote for me. When the result was released, that demobilized soldier was very angry. He even went to question our leaders. Soon afterwards, he left our school and transferred to the factory's propaganda department."[20]

Ni's experience shows that, due to the existence of private canvassing, the secret ballot did not help to avoid the segmental effect in the course of competition between workers for the wage increase. In fact, mutual support based on personal relationships further strengthened the internal solidarity of the existing subgroups and made the difference among groups more visible.[21] As the informant Mr. Yin Qiming summarized, "in my opinion, the 40% policy had a very negative effect on the workers' solidarity. It unintentionally led to a series of conflicts among workers, between workers and leaders, and also among leaders (*qunzhong dou qunzhogn, qunzhong dou ganbu, ganbu dou ganbu*)."[22]

To sum up, over an extended period of day-to-day interaction inside and outside the workshops, Jinjiang Factory workers had developed their perceptions and attitudes of one group toward another. In other words, through their daily activities, the notion of "group belonging" gradually materialized as a visible boundary differentiating and dividing the working class in the factory. As a result, workers in each group were more willing to build their social relationships within the group they belonged to.

4.4   INTERCONNECTED SOCIAL NETWORKS IN THE JINJIANG FACTORY

Living in a relatively isolated site, Jinjiang Factory workers were highly dependent on the factory in building social relationships. A good example is the informant Tan Yi's kinship network:

As Fig. 4.2 shows, ten families were included in Tan Yi's kinship network and each is denoted by the first letter of their family name. My interviewee Tan Yi and his wife are denoted by T1 and W1. T2 and T3 are two brothers of Tan Yi and they married the daughters of the heads of the finance department and quality inspection department respectively, who are denoted by D1 and S2. S2 had a brother, S1, who married the daughter of a senior worker L; he was the nephew of Q, both of whom worked in the Matching Parts Workshop. Q's daughter Q2 was working in the dining hall, and her husband was a cadre working in the general office. Q2's elder brother Q1 was a worker in the Machining Workshop. His wife Z1 was working with her father Z in the Heat Treatment Workshop. Tan

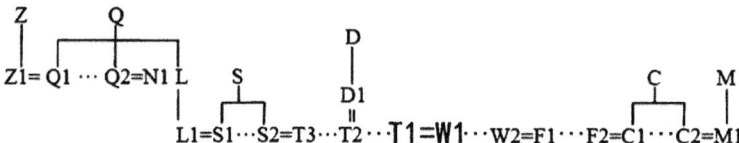

Fig. 4.2   Tan Yi's kinship network in Jinjiang Factor. (Notes: In this figure, all the capital letters are the first letter of people's family name. "=" denotes a marital relationship; "..." denotes siblings; "_" linking different capital letters indicates people across generations, but not necessarily a parent–child relationship)

Yi's wife W1 was working in the factory's kindergarten, and her younger brother, W2, was in charge of marketing in the Instrument Production Workshop. W2's wife, F1, worked in the Assembly Workshop. Her elder sister, F2, working in the Forging and Casting Workshop, got married to a worker, C1, in the Machining Workshop. C1's elder brother C2 married the daughter of the deputy director of Jinjiang Factory. C1 and C2's father was a senior worker transferred from Shanghai.

The example of Tan Yi's kinship network may, of course, show an extreme case in Jinjiang Factory and not all workers were in kinship networks like this. But it was certainly not exceptional either. Otherwise, the workers would not have felt so strongly the tangled relationships among families.

> The social relationship in the factory was so complicated! Every family had twisted roots and gnarled branches (*pangen cuojie*). It was true that if you pulled one hair, the whole body would be affected (*qian yifa er dong quanshen*). So you had to make any decision with great caution. You would never know who would be affected in the end.[23]

> Living together for a long time, every family in our factory had a close relationship with each other. Workers always laughingly described it as "one twig shakes, hundreds would follow" (*yizhi dong baizhi yao*)[24]

Chen and Fu vividly illustrated that no worker in Jinjiang Factory was an atomized individual. Instead, each belonged to a family group composed of different nuclear families. As a result, the initially atomized working class in the factory was gradually transformed into a corporate organization by interfamily marriages.

However, these social relationships were not built at random, whereby any two workers were able to establish ties with each other. Specifically, in Jinjiang Factory, friendships and marriages were more likely to occur between workers of the same group. As some sociologists have argued, "friends assess others in a similar way. If A and B have positive feelings about each other, and person B has positive feelings about person C, then person A will also know and have positive feelings about person C." Over time, the interconnected social networks were weaved in each group of workers. This phenomenon can be roughly illustrated as in Fig. 4.3. In Fig. 4.3, workers were divided in terms of their group belongings. In each

Demobilized Soldiers

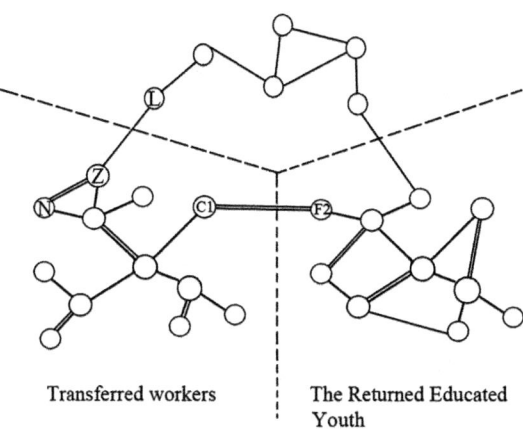

Transferred workers ┊ The Returned Educated
┊ Youth

Fig. 4.3 Interconnected social networks in Jinjiang Factory. (Notes: "=" denotes marriages; "_" denotes friendship or relatives beyond immediate family members (husband and wife); "N" represents the husband of Zhu Guiqin ("Z"); "L" represents the interviewee LanQingshan; "F2" and "C1" are the members in Tan Yi's kinship network shown in Fig. 4.2)

group, the social relationships were intensive and thus workers were connected to each other one way or another. However, these intimate relationships were rarely constructed across different groups.

The interconnected social networks were found during the interviews as well. In the process of snowballing interviewees, I noticed a tendency for the nominators and the nominees to share the same group belongings in the factory. It was very rare to get a transferred worker to recommend a demobilized soldier or a Returned Educated Youth worker and vice versa. Based on the assumption that people are more likely to nominate the person with whom they had the closest relationship, I infer that the building of friendships mainly happened among workers of the same label. To check the robustness of this inference, I asked interviewees to list the friends who they contacted and interacted with most frequently. All the names provided by each interviewee in the end belonged to people with the same background. For example, Liu Chengmin mentioned five men in total, all of whom were *Jixiaosheng* who graduated from the same technical school as him in Shanghai.[25] One possible way to bring the transferred workers together with the Returned Educated Youths and the demobilized soldiers was through the master–apprentice relationship. But the results of the interviews indicate that the effect of such a relationship needs to be assessed on a case-by-case basis. Almost all the workers interviewed expressed respect for their masters, and some reported that they would send good wishes and gifts to their masters at every festival. But only one admitted that such relationships would eventually develop into close friendship. In some cases, on the contrary, the master–apprentice relationship could even reinforce the existing stereotypes of a particular group. The aforementioned LanQingshan's experience was a typical example.

Marriages were also more likely to occur within the group of a certain label. Among all the interviewees, only three had cross-group marriages.[26] The rest, except for the demobilized soldiers, married colleagues with the same background. Most of the demobilized soldiers had already been married prior to their employment in the factory and their wives stayed at home doing farm work. In reality, of course, the pattern of marriages among workers was not as neat as it seems in theory. If we look at the whole family tree of a worker in the factory, it is not surprising to find a distant relative coming from a different group. Take Tan Yi's kinship network as an example again: Tan Yi is a demobilized soldier but his wife's brother's wife's sister's husband's father is a senior worker transferred from Shanghai.

In fact, there were similar exceptions in respect of the building of friendships. The close relationship between two of the interviewees, LanQingshan and Zhu Guiqin, was a good example. As mentioned earlier, LanQingshan was a demobilized soldier who frequently encountered friction with the transferred Shanghai workers. But he had quite a good impression of Zhu Guiqin. He told me that "Fellow Zhu (*Zhu shifu*) was not like other Shanghai workers. She was kind to me and taught me a lot in the Instrument Production Workshop."[27] Given Lan's frequent unpleasant experiences with many other Shanghai workers, his friendship with Zhu appeared especially precious. Lan visited Zhu regularly even after their retirements, though his home was more than an hour away by car.

In a word, even though there were occasionally "strong ties" across the boundary of different groups, these do not challenge the general pattern that workers of one group were reluctant to establish kinship and intimate friendship with colleagues from another.

4.5   CONTRASTING SOCIAL RELATIONS IN URBAN SOEs AND JINJIANG FACTORY

The phenomenon of clanization in urban work units has been discussed in some previous studies. However, the features of clanization mentioned in the existing literature are quite different from those in the Third Line Enterprises. In his pioneering work, Lu Feng conceptualizes clanization in terms of the relationship between individual and organization. According to Lu (1989), the work unit shared many similarities with traditional Chinese families. First, members of the work unit must be subordinate to the paternal authority of the organization; second, an individual's obligation to the organization was more important than his/her rights; third, the organization should take full responsibility for taking care of their members' welfare. These three features, mentioned by Lu, could actually be found in every factory, including the Third Line Enterprises. As a result, even though Lu offers an insightful conceptualization of clanization, this concept is not very meaningful because it is essentially a constant.

One way to address this limitation is to shift the focus from the relationship between individual and organization to that between individuals. Dittmer and Lü (1996) have made a significant contribution in this direction. According to these authors, clanization is a relatively new form of informal relationship in the post-Mao period, which typically occurred in state agencies and other administrative organs (p. 259). In these clanized work units, many cadres were working with their direct family members or people with lineage ties in the same department.

We can basically identify two features of clanization from the work of Dittmer and Lü (pp. 259–60). First, clanization is a political phenomenon, created by the holding of power, as shown in the evidence provided by the authors:

> In the county government agencies of a remote northern province, 68 of 148 cadres who held important positions had relatives working in the same agencies; of these, 27 children worked with their parents, four couples shared the same office, and 23 people had cousins, uncles, brothers-in-law, or godchildren working in the same agencies.

For the powerless ordinary workers, the phenomenon of clanization is relatively rare. According to the authors, except for instances of *dingti* (replacement of retired workers with their children or relatives) or *neizhao* (recruitment of the children or relatives of internal workers), ordinary workers had almost no opportunity to get their family members a job in the same factory.

Second, clanization among cadres took on a single-centered hierarchical structure with the family member holding the highest power at the top. Usually, the member at the top of the hierarchy would hire employees based on kinship. As a result, different families were relatively independent from each other with clear demarcation lines between them. This structural feature was vividly described by the popular satire: "pop-son bureau, hubby-wife section, son pours water for dad, grandson drives for granny, spouses share an office desk" (*fuzi chu, fuqi ke, erzi daocha laodie he, sunzi dang siji, yuanyang gongyong bangongzhuo*) (Dittmer and Lü 1996, p. 259).

Nevertheless, clanization in the Third Line Enterprises differed from Dittmer and Lü's account. First, clanization in these Enterprises was not a political phenomenon based on power. Instead, it was by and large a social phenomenon based on the marriage between two workers and, later, two families, regardless of the power of their positions in the factory. In other words, it was not a nepotistic but a marital relationship. Hence, if clanization in urban work units was an intentional consequence of power, then clanization in the Third Line Enterprises could be considered an unintended result of isolation.

In fact, the factory's isolated location was not the only factor causing clanization. The political ends of the Third Line Enterprises further intensified this phenomenon. Due to their high level of secrecy, unlike the factories in cities, the Third Line Enterprises relied more on the *neizhao* policy for recruitment in order to guarantee the political credibility of new workers. Candidates related to current workers, in the form of brothers, sisters, brothers-in-law, sisters-in-law, nephews, nieces and cousins, were prioritized for recruitment by internal recommendation (*neibu tuijian*). As a result, in the latter stages of the Third Line Construction, marriage between two workers was actually a marriage between two big families.

Clanization due to intermarriage among families produced the second different feature of the social structure in Third Line Enterprises. The structural difference of clanization between urban factories and Third Line Enterprises is illustrated in Fig. 4.4. In the single-centered hierarchical structure shown by the solid dots in Fig. 4.4, every family is an independent interest community, centered around the member who possessed the greatest power. In the multi-centered radiant structure shown by the

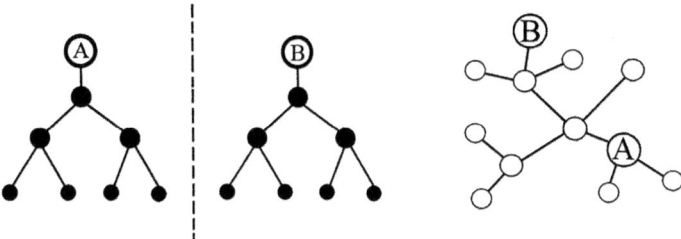

Fig. 4.4   Social relations of two different structural features

hollow dots in Fig. 4.4, every family is situated in an intricate and complex social network, its boundary demarcated not in terms of each independent family but by the group labels. As a result, compared to their urban counterparts, Third Line workers were living in a bigger and more compact net, like the gentle but mobile surface of water in a deep pond. Once any part of the pond was disturbed, ripples would spread out.

4.6   CONCLUSION

This chapter has explained the emotional basis for toleration. Due to living in the mountains, isolated from the outside world, workers at Jinjiang Factory sought their friends and marital partners within the factory. In this process, they became interconnected in one way or another. However, this interconnection did not occur in a random manner. It was constrained within the subgroup that the worker belonged to. Generally speaking, workers in Jinjiang Factory were divided into three groups: transferred workers, Returned Educated Youths, and demobilized soldiers. This division of workers was strengthened by their occupational niches in the factory and reinforced in day-to-day interactions inside and outside the workshop.

A direct consequence of the interconnected social networks was the complication of interpersonal relationships in the factory. The formal relationships of colleagues or between superiors and subordinates were at the same time intermingled with informal ones, such as friends, relatives, or even husband and wife. In this sense, the boundary between family and factory was blurred. In this context, group leaders and managers in the workshop tended to implement the formal policies loosely.

Admittedly, the relatives of managers sometimes could be placed in an easier and more comfortable position at the workplace. However, this preferential treatment did not impede the development of group leaders' toleration. From Tan's family tree, it can be seen that the social networks in Jinjiang Factory were so interconnected that even an ordinary worker could be somehow related to a director or a party secretary of a workshop.

It is worth noting that the segmentation of workers at Jinjiang Factory could not be fully explained by Perry's "politics of places" (Perry 1993; Hershatter 1986). According to Perry, workers in Shanghai prior to the establishment of the People's Republic of China were divided in terms of their respective places of origin. In Jinjiang Factory, however, both the Returned Educated Youths and the demobilized soldiers were natives of Sichuan, but were separated into two different subgroups. These two groups of people shared the same origin, but had different backgrounds due to state policy. In this sense, the segmentation of Shanghai workers was in fact a result of *societal* mobilization, which was realized through two intermediate social actors—the guild and gangs—while the segmentation of workers at Jinjiang Factory was a consequence of *state* mobilization. The transferred workers, Returned Educated Youths, and demobilized soldiers were respectively related to a particular state-initiated political movement, and these identities were being continuously strengthened by a series of socioeconomic policies.

NOTES

1. From 1951 to the late 1980s, Chinese SOEs applied the Eight-Grade wage system to workers and the Twenty-Two-Grade wage system to managers. Workers were classified in different grades according to their seniority and skill level. The first grade indicated the most inexperienced and lowest skilled worker, while the eighth grade referred to the most experienced and highest skilled. In practice, every worker could be upgraded step by step in a certain (fixed) number of years.
2. Interview with LanQingshan.
3. In many previous studies, women were usually seen as an unskilled group of labor compared to their male counterparts (Deyo 1989; Perry 1993).
4. Interview with Cao Mingshen.
5. Interview with Zhu Guiqin.
6. Interview with Zhu Guiqin.
7. Interview with Zhu Guiqin.

8. Interview with Liu Chengmin.
9. Interestingly, none of the workers mentioned *mahjong* as their favorite game in their leisure time. One reason might be that, in the official discourse of the factory, *mahjong* was regarded as a gambling activity, enjoyment of which signified a waste of one's time and even a lack of morality.
10. The scholars of production politics associate labor politics with the labor process (Burawoy 1979; Edwards 1979; Sabel 1982; Hanagan and Stephenson 1986; Edwards 1986).
11. Interview with Zhu Guiqin.
12. Interview with Zhu Guiqin.
13. Interview with Liu Chengmin.
14. Interview with LanQingshan.
15. Interview with LanQingshan.
16. Interview with LanQingshan.
17. Interview with LanQingshan.
18. Interview with Tan Yi.
19. It was recognized by informants Cao Mingshen (Director of the Matching Parts Workshop), Wang Lin and Fu Qianwei (Directors of the Machinery Workshop at different times), and Huang Limin, a section chief in the Instrument Production Workshop.
20. Interview with Ni Tongzheng.
21. It is worth noting that the wage increase reform in the 1980s did not very much influence the group internal governance because the members in a certain group were quite homogeneous in terms of their origins. As mentioned above in this chapter, workers' job opportunities in the factory were closely associated with their origins.
22. Interview with Yin Qiming.
23. Interview with Chen Youbai.
24. Interview with Fujianwei.
25. Interview with Liu Chengmin.
26. These are Liu Chengmin, Cao Mingshen and Lu Liqiang. These three men were all from Shanghai, but married to local women.
27. Interview with Lan Qingshan.

REFERENCES

Burawoy, Michael. 1979. *Manufacturing Consent: Changes in the Labor Process Under Monopoly Capitalism*, Chicago: University of Chicago Press.

Blecher, Marc. 1984. Peasant Labor for Urban Industry: Temporary Contract Labor, Urban-Rural Balance and Class Relations in a Chinese County, in Maxwell, Neville and Bruce McFarlane, eds. *China's Changed Road to Development*, Oxford: Pergamon Press, 109–123.

Bourdieu, Pierre. 1991. Sport and Social Class, in Chandra Mukerji and Michael Schudson, eds. *Rethinking Popular Culture: Contemporary Perspective in Cultural Studies*, Berkeley: University of California Press, 369–70.

Deyo, Frederic C. 1989. *Beneath the Miracle: Labor Subordination in the New Asian Industrialism*, Berkeley: University of California Press.

Dittmer, Lowell and Xiaobo Lü. 1996 (March). Personal Politics in the Chinese Danwei under Reform, *Asian Survey*, 36 (3):246–267.

Edwards, Richard. 1979. *Contested Terrain: The Transformation of the Workplace in the Twentieth Century*, London: Basic Books.

Edwards, P. K. 1986. *Conflict at Work: A Materialist Analysis of Workplace Relations*, Oxford: Basil Blackwell.

Gold, Thomas B. 1980 (December). Back to the City: the Return of Shanghai's Educated Youth, *The China Quarterly*, 84:755–770.

Glickman, Rose. 1984. *Russian Factory Women: Workplace and Society, 1880–1914*, Berkeley: The University of California Press.

Honing, Emily. 1986. *Sisters and Strangers: Women in the Shanghai Cotton Mills, 1919–1949*, Stanford: Stanford University Press.

Hanagan, Michael and Charles Stephenson (eds.) 1986. *Confrontation, Class Consciousness, and the Labor Process: Studies in Proletarian Class Formation*, Westport: Greenwood Press.

Hershatter, Gail. 1986. *The Workers of Tianjin, 1900–1949*, Stanford: Stanford University Press.

Jinjiang Oil Pump and Oil Nozzle Factory. 1983 (December). *Documents of the Report on the Reorganization of the Enterprise*.

Lu, Feng. 1989. Danwei: A Unique Form of Social Organization, *Chinese Social Science*, 1:71–88.

Lin, Kun-Chin. 2009. Class Formation or Fragmentation? Allegiances and Divisions Among Managers and Workers in State-Owned Enterprises, in Gold B. Thomas and etc., ed. *Laid-off Workers in a Workers' State: Unemployment with Chinese Characteristics*, NY: Palgrave Macmillan, 61–94.

McLaren, Anne. 1979 (July). The Educated Youth Return: The Poster Campaign in Shanghai from November 1978 to March 1979, *The Australian Journal of Chinese Affairs*, 2:1–20.

Perry, Elizabeth. 1993. *Shanghai on Strike: The Politics of Chinese Labor*, Stanford: Stanford University Press.

Perry, Elizabeth. 1994 (March). Shanghai's Strike Wave of 1957. *The China Quarterly*, 137:1–27.

Sabel, Charles F. 1982. *Work and Politics: The Division of Labor in Industry*, New York: Cambridge University Press.

The Sichuan Provincial Department of Machinery Industry. 1985. *A Report on the Recognition of 30 Large-Scale Enterprises in the Machinery Industry of Our Province*, the Government Document No. (85) 059.

Tilly, Louise A. 1986. Paths of Proletarianization: Organization of Production, Sexual Division of Labor, and Women's Collective Action, in Leacock, Eleanor and Helen I. Safa, eds. *Women's Work: Development and the Division of Labor by Gender*, South Hadley, MA: Bergin & Garvey, 25–40.

Walder, Andrew G. 1987 (March). Wage Reform and the Web of Factory Interests, *The China Quarterly*, 109:22–41.

CHAPTER 5

The Context of Toleration (3): Workers' Control on Production

In Jinjiang Factory, the tolerating strategy was also a compromise on the part of the group leaders. This compromise was a result of workers' control over production, rooted in two institutional features: the workers' permanent employment status and the occupational immobility within the factory. The compromise between group leaders and workers at Jinjiang Factory reveals that the style of management is not merely a product of macro-structural conditions. It is also a reflection of the group leaders' subtle maneuverings in their handling of various circumstances in day-to-day activities. Simply put, it represents the leaders' accommodation of the combined and intertwined effects of the state, the production process, and social relations.

This chapter begins with a discussion of the permanent employment status. I will argue that it is this status that provided the institutional basis for the workers' ability to violate the formal rules. In the second and third sections, I will introduce two direct consequences of occupational immobility within the factory: the group leaders' preferences to maintain personal reputations and friendly relationships with others, and the development of workers' control over daily pace of production. Basically, the workers' control contained three elements. First, workers were autonomous in ordering the sequence of processing among different parts. Second, they also had the autonomy to balance their quota tasks among different parts. And, third, workers could expand their autonomy over the rate of production by making use of the uncoordinated actions or plans

99
C. Chen, *Toleration*, New Perspectives on Chinese Politics and Society, https://doi.org/10.1007/978-981-10-8941-1_5

among different factory departments, workshops, working groups, and even individuals. The final section offers some conclusions.

5.1   PERMANENT EMPLOYMENT STATUS

On a fundamental level, permanent employment status provided the institutional basis for workers' violations of the formal rules. Conventional wisdom associates permanent employment status with the low efficiency of Chinese SOEs. According to these works, workers in SOEs had no incentive to work hard because their performance had little effect on their income and the factory management even had no right to fire employees unless they committed a crime (Walder 1986; Lu 1989; Li 1993; Liu 2002). In Jinjiang Factory, the permanency of employment status provided the workers with the leverage for dealing with the managers.

The permanent employment status of workers at Jinjiang Factory lasted until 1999, when the first round of lay-offs was carried out. Prior to that, it had long been one of the most crucial factors impeding managers' discretion in the workshop. In Tan Yi's working diary, Ma Jie was perhaps the biggest troublemaker and gave the factory's management a big headache. No matter what he did in the factory, including shirking, bullying, and vandalism, the management could do nothing but try to educate and reeducate him. Even though he was diagnosed with a mental illness, the factory lacked any better ways to deal with his problem. The following lengthy extract from Tan Yi's working diary records the factory's difficulty in dealing with this troublemaker.

July 6, 1987, Monday (Factory Friday[1]) Sunny
Ma Jie beat up Wang Yongxin. The workshop decided to give him administrative sanction and sent him to the hospital for treatment of his mental illness.

July 21, 1987, Tuesday (Factory Saturday) Cloudy
I talked to Ma Jie and asked him to acknowledge his mistake, write a self-criticism and make an apology.

August 8, 1987, Saturday (Factory Wednesday) Sunny
I talked to Ma Jie. He agreed to write a self-criticism and make an apology in the group meeting.

August 9, 1987, Sunday (Factory Thursday) Partially Cloudy

Ma Jie beat up XuYingshi. The workshop decided to return his personnel calmly to the Department of Human Resources and ask them to transfer him to another position in the factory.

August 15, 1987, Saturday (Factory Wednesday) Sunny

I talked to Ma Jie together with factory deputy director Yu and the factory's Party secretary, Zhang. He did not acknowledge his mistake but blamed the leaders of the workshop and other colleagues. After two hours of heart-to-heart talk, he decided to make a self-criticism in the workshop tomorrow morning. The workshop made a decision that, as long as he did not make the mistake again, the workshop would keep him in his present position.

August 22, 1987, Saturday (Factory Wednesday) Cloudy

Ma Jie's mother arrived at the factory today. We exchanged our opinions on the problem of Ma Jie. We also talked to him patiently in an attempt to make him aware of his mistakes.

September 19, 1987, Saturday (Factory Wednesday) Cloudy

Ma Jie quarreled with some workers in the Machining Workshop.

September 21, 1987, Monday (Factory Friday) Sunny

I talked to Ma Jie and tried to educate him and help him.

November 24, 1987, Tuesday (Factory Saturday) Cloudy

Ma Jie fought with Liu Hanji. According to the factory's investigation, Ma Jie landed the first blow on Liu Hanji. Then Liu Hanji fought back. The cause of the fight was that Ma Jie smoked in the workshop and Liu attempted to stop him. The factory leaders will talk to Ma Jie next Monday.

December 4, 1987, Friday (Factory Tuesday) Cloudy

For no reason, Ma Jie struck the door of the Quality Control Room in the workshop with an iron bar. The door was badly damaged, with a one-foot crack on it. Nobody seems to have set him off, actually. According to Ma Jie himself, "There was a fire within my body and I just wanted to release it". It seemed that the workshop could not have him anymore.

Ma Jie's case showed that the factory could not easily fire any of its permanent workers. Womack also recognized the empowering effect of permanent employment. He responds to Walder by pointing out that his "over-concentration on state power overlooks the concrete limits on leadership discretion, ignores the informality of power in small-scale, stable situations, and produces a skewed and unrealistic view of workplace interrelationships" (Womack 1991, p. 323). The crucial concrete limit on leadership discretion, argued Womack, is "the context of permanent employment in state Enterprises", which "has been seen as a benefit by the workers, and it limits the leadership in its choice of sanctions" (p. 322). Hence, the constrained group leaders were barely capable of exerting their power in a *coercive* way and it would be unrealistic for them to expect full obedience from their workers. If any request was perceived as unsatisfying, it was very likely to be contested by their members through a series of acts of non-cooperation. As Liu Chengmin, who used to be the group leader in the Heat Treatment Workshop, recalled:

> The job of being a group leader was quite difficult … Many demobilized soldiers and Returned Educated Youth were not well-educated and their skills were also poor. So the leaders of our workshop always encouraged us to organize some skills training activities. I used to attempt to initiate some, but all of them failed. My group workers refused to participate in the skill training activities. They said I started these activities just out of my personal interest. They speculated that it was my way to accumulate political capital, by which I could be promoted in the future. Besides, they did not want their leisure time to be taken up by these boring activities.[2]

Liu Chengmin's experience can also be found in Tan Yi's working dairy. Interestingly, Tan's record of this anecdote is more dramatic than Liu's oral description:

> 23rd December, 1987 Sunday (Factory Thursday) Rainy
>
> Morning: The Director [of the Heat Treatment Workshop] and I had a heart-to-heart talk with Liu Chengmin. Liu submitted his resignation application in the morning. He felt it was too difficult to be a group leader. He felt very aggrieved at not being understood by his member workers. He cried bitterly. The Director and I consoled him first, and went on to analyze and explain the difficulties he encountered. Liu's experience revealed some common problems that existed in our workshop: the cooperation between different groups, the cooperation within the group, the implementation of the group regulation and the management skills of the group leaders and so on. Next year, the workshop should focus on the project of working group improvement.

Tan's diary shows that Liu's experience was by no means an uncommon occurrence in Jinjiang Factory. In these working groups, member workers had never been a powerless group subordinating to their immediate leaders.

5.2   Job Immobility and Preference for Personal Reputation

The balancing effect of member workers was further strengthened by the relative immobility across jobs within the factory. As in the case of inter-firm transfer, mobility across different jobs within the factory was also rare in Jinjiang Factory. This phenomenon can be seen in Zhu Guiqin's explanation of her pace of work when she temporarily provided help in another workshop.

> Some shifted workers' hard work might increase the production quota of the whole section they were in. It was not a big deal for our shifted workers because we only worked there for a while, but the front workers had to work there for their whole life![3]

Job immobility defined the nature of the game between the group leaders and their member workers. Essentially, it was an infinitely repeated game over an infinite horizon. In this game, even though the group leaders theoretically had the authority to implement the regulations issued by the upper level management regardless of their members' feelings, as mentioned above, in practice they had to face the challenges of non-cooperation from their member workers whenever those measures were perceived as unsatisfying. In other words, in this repeated game, the group leaders and member workers were playing a form of "tit-for-tat". As predicted by the models of repeated games, cooperation can constitute a stable equilibrium in such games because future gains from mutual cooperation can counter the short-term incentive to cheat (Axelrod 1984). Indeed, the group leaders at Jinjiang Factory usually had their own ways of compromising the interests of their bosses and member workers, which will be discussed in detail later in this chapter.[4]

The job immobility in the factory defined not only the nature of the game but also the players' preference structure. Previous studies on Chinese labor policy have failed to consider group leaders' preferences within concrete social structures. Usually, they simply equate the group leaders' preferences with those of the factory managers—namely, the factory's output or profits—and have overlooked the independent role of the group leaders. Of course, the group leaders' strong preference would be to meet and even exceed the production target. But it had never been their single most important preference, especially when we take into account their specific situations. Due to the job immobility in Jinjiang Factory, the group leaders greatly valued the *reputations* they held among others. Furthermore, their isolated condition and relatively closed life also increased the weight of reputation, which was not necessarily any less important than their completion of the production task:

> You could not apply the formal rules very strictly. Otherwise, you must be resented by your member workers. In such a small factory site, we met regularly and frequently, and some of us were even neighbors. It was unwise not to get on well with your colleagues.[5]

> It was not much good talking about formal discipline or the Thoughts of Mao Zedong to your workers. That would quickly stimulate their antipathy against you and ultimately destroy your prestige in the working group. If that happened, how could your work get done? So the first lesson of being a group leader is to learn how to get on well with your member workers.[6]

Fu and Cao's descriptions suggest the importance of the relationship inside the working group. In fact, the group leaders' authority was sometimes also constrained by the complicated social ties outside the working groups, as Chen Youbai recalled:

> You had to make any decision with great caution, because you would never know who would be affected in the end. Let me give you an example to show the complexity. In our Heat Treatment Workshop, the most regular number of workers was around 40. But do you know what was the maximum number of workers we ever had? It was more than 80! People all knew that the work in our workshop was relatively less laborious than the other front workshops, so many of them liked to send their brothers, sisters, sons or daughters to our workshop. Eventually, there were so many relationships in the workshop you need to think about. I must admit that the complicated relationships in the workshop did affect my work and even the factory's regular production.[7]

According to other informants, Chen had the reputation in the factory of *laohaoren*, meaning that he avoided offending anybody. Chen's easy-going and gentle personality probably made him more constrained by social ties than others, which in a way called into question the relevance of his experience to others. However, in light of the other two informants' statements, it would be difficult to deny that the complicated social relations constrained the workshop managers.

5.3   Job Immobility and Workers' Control on Production

The group leaders' discretion over the production line was also greatly challenged by the workers' autonomy over their day-to-day pace of work. This important leverage of labor had, however, been overlooked in previous studies of Chinese labor. In analyzing workers in SOEs, previous studies concentrated on either their obedience under the socialist authoritarian regime (Walder 1986; Zhao and Nichols 1996; Gold 1980; McLaren 1979; Perry 1994) or their sporadically organized protests ignited by major policy changes, such as the policy to repatriate the Educated Youths and the market-oriented reforms (Chen 2003, 2006; Cai 2006; Lee 2007; Hurst 2009). In the studies focusing on the workers' obedience, scholars attempt to discover the various means of control in the factory, while those focusing on protests endeavor to find the opportunities for and organizational resources in the course of protest mobilization. The truth is, however, that Chinese workers in socialist Enterprises were neither obedient in nature nor only troublesome in sporadically organized movements. They could express their dissatisfaction by employing their "weapons of the weak" in everyday production. "It is commonplace that, even under slavery, workers have means of slowing down the pace of work" (Edwards 1986, p. 73). This autonomy undoubtedly existed in socialist factories as well. Moreover, it was strengthened by the workers' job immobility in the factory, as mentioned earlier.

An unintended consequence of job immobility was the strengthening of workers' autonomy over the pace of work. During apprenticeship, workers were usually trained in skills that were specific to a particular machine shop, or even a particular section. Thus, by matching workers trained in a particular skill to specific positions in the workshop, the factory could not only reduce the costs of retraining but also enhance the efficiency of production. However, the factory was not the only party that benefited from this policy. According to the interviewees, they also preferred to stay in one job, not only because they had limited skill profiles but also because it enabled them to have better control over the working process. Seniority in one position provided them complete knowledge of every detail of their work: the process of material distribution, the condition of tools and machines, the personality of colleagues, and so on. All of this "tacit knowledge" related to production could not have been more valuable to the workers because it earned them more salary and more free time.

Overall, the workers' autonomy over their daily production could be viewed from at least three perspectives. First, they were autonomous in ordering the sequence of processing for different parts. Take workers of the Machining Workshop as an example: except for the fuel-injection nozzle, which was produced in the Matching Parts Workshop, the Machining Workshop was in charge of processing more than 400 different parts, such as the pump, camshaft, and front and back covers. These different products were assigned to ten production groups, and workers in each group were assigned specific tasks in terms of types of work—such as lathing, grinding, drilling, milling, and planing—rather than the type of parts. Therefore, although the workers were assigned specific tasks, it did not mean that they were merely responsible for processing a particular part. Every month, as long as they were able to meet the required quota, the group leaders would not interfere with their processing order; it was entirely the workers' own business. This autonomy of workers caused a lot of trouble for the group leaders, as the leader of the camshaft group complained:

> We were assigned tasks in terms of type of work. For every type of work, a worker usually had more than one type of part to work on. You see, this raised the important issue of processing order. In the workshop, we did not have a rule specifying each worker's processing sequence, and I think it was actually impossible to make such a rule because the actual situations were usually very flexible and changeable. Sometimes you had to speed up your production of some parts for the Assembly Workshop; sometimes you could even slow down your work on some parts, since no time slot for heat treatment was available. The responsibility for coordination always fell on our shoulders; the member workers could not be bothered to think about this. They were more willing to first process the parts that had a less strict quota time, or with a low risk of wastage, and they usually attempted to avoid or procrastinate those otherwise. How to effectively mobilize them, to be honest, completely depended on whether you had the talent.[8]

Second, the workers also had the autonomy to vary their quota task between different parts. On paper, only the director and the leader of the workshop's planning group had the right to adjust the quota between different products in response to the changing production situation. In practice, however, the rank-and-file workers used this autonomy to take advantage of the rules' limitations. According to factory regulations, every worker had a standard requirement to work 208 hours per month and bonuses would only be given for extra working hours over 208. How much bonus a worker could earn therefore mostly depended on how many extra hours he/she could work. The implementation of this regulation hinged on the feasibility of calculating the workers' actual working hours. Generally speaking, the calculation was based on the number of different parts workers actually completed. As mentioned earlier, workers assigned a specific task that usually had more than one type of part to process. The different structures and designs meant that, although workers were doing identical work, the processing time for each type of part was nevertheless very different. Thus, the actual number of working hours was the sum of the working time on each type of part, which was defined by the "quota time". For example, if a worker lathed 200 front covers and 300 back covers a month, and the determined standard times for lathing a front cover and back cover were respectively 20 and 30 minutes, then this worker's actual working hours in a month were $[(20 \times 200) + (30 \times 300)] / 60 = 216.7$.

The quota time for each process on each part was determined by the factory. In December every year, based on the factory's production records and with reference to other factories' standards, the Department of Human Resources determined the quota time for each part for the following year's production. In this way, the quota time for regularly produced parts could be more precisely determined, taking into consideration the time necessary for production preparation and physical recovery. As for newly developed parts and products, due to the lack of previous production records, the quota time was less precise and usually longer than what the technological prediction had suggested. As mentioned above, the factory's determined quota time was subject to change. In fact, it could be readjusted by the workshop quota setters according to the specific conditions in their workshops.

As can be seen, the method used to calculate the actual working hours only took account of the total amount of time a worker eventually spent on the task and failed to take into consideration the type of part being worked on. The workers were therefore able individually to vary their working hours between different parts. An effective ratio method could not only help them complete the required 208 basic working hours as quickly as possible but also allow them to earn more bonuses than others. Driven by this potential economic interest, many workers at Jinjiang Factory were from time to time tempted to make use of this autonomy. This can be seen from the following statement by the Director of the Machinery Workshop:

> In 1984, I was transferred from the factory's General Office and became the Director of the Machinery Workshop. For quite a long time, this workshop, despite being one of the most important, had failed to complete the production task assigned by the factory. This was why my leaders transferred me from the office to the front line of production. Before I came to this shop, I guessed something inappropriate might exist in the quota-setting process. After a period of close contact with the group leaders and workers, I realized that my previous guess was completely wrong. There was nothing inappropriate with the quota requirement, and there was no problem with the workers' production capacity either. It was our problematic incentive system that resulted in the production failure. The only thing that worried the workers was their ultimate working hours. They did not care about the problem of coordination with others or whether the workshop could meet the factory's requirements. As a result, the workers were very likely to produce 600 or even more of some easily processed part only 500 of which were enough to meet the target. This was a rational choice for them because, if they produced more of the easily processed parts, then they could save much effort on the difficult ones. For the factory, however, this was damaging. On one hand, they wasted a lot of precious materials and, on the other, they also delayed the subsequent work of another workshop.[9]

Third, workers could also expand their autonomy over the pace of production by taking advantage of the uncoordinated actions or plans of different factory departments, workshops, working groups, and even individuals. The factory workshops were not operated separately, but in a coordinated way. The progress of production could be slowed down due to delayed supply of raw materials, no available time slot for heat treatment, or tardiness in the making of required instruments. Any uncoordinated action would definitely harm the factory's interests, whereas it provided the workers with opportunities to seek free time. This was because they could use these organizational defects as reasonable excuses for slowing down the pace of production.

Although uncoordinated actions between different departments seldom occurred, those between different workers were frequent. One fact that could not be ignored was that it was not possible for workers doing different types of work to finish their work at the same time. This led to the very natural consequence that, for example, when a lathe worker finished his work on the bases of delivery valves and was prepared to lathe the joint screws, the screws would, however, still be being processed by another drilling worker. This uncoordinated action between workers created a production-free period for the faster workers while they waited for the next work. This period in the workshop was known by workers as "waiting for a job time" (*denggong shijian*). In cases where this delay was quite long due to particular organizational problems in different groups or sections, these faster workers could even gain a day or half a day off.

This coordination problem was especially serious in the Machining Workshop. As mentioned above, more than 400 parts (excluding standard parts such as the screw and screw cap) were processed in this workshop, and each required a certain number of processing steps. For example, the processing of a camshaft consisted of 43 steps. Efficient coordination of the 43 steps among different groups and workers had always been a big challenge for both the section chiefs and the group leaders. To make thing worse, as the number of parts awaiting processing increased, coordination became more challenging than ever before. This ever-present challenge to the management, however, benefited the workers as it gave them more opportunities to seek free time. This phenomenon was indirectly recalled by the Director of the Machining Workshop:

"Before taking up my post in the workshop, I actually carried out some investigations into the conditions of the place where I was about to work. I did this because I did not have much working experience in the front production workshops. I knew almost nothing about it. Privately, I was told by the previous workshop director that the end of every month was a really difficult time. At that time, many workers would come to the previous director's office and hurl the question 'On what basis did you give me so much less bonus than the others?' As they asked, some of them even glared fiercely and pounded the desk angrily."

"Why did this problem happen?" I asked. "Wasn't there the record of working hours as the basis [for calculation]?"

"Working hours were just one determinant of one's ultimate bonus, actually. The quality of their work, the maintenance of the machine and the safety of production and so on would also be considered. In addition, they could also bargain with the director, claiming that it was the interrupted provision of work that slowed down their own pace. It was therefore a management problem, but not the workers'."[10]

It is worth mentioning that the workers in the Instrument Production Workshop and the Heat Treatment Workshop exploited their autonomy differently, due to their respective ways of production organization. In the Instrument Production Workshop, workers were independently responsible for the production of a certain set of instruments and did not have to coordinate with others within the workshops. This independence did not actually reduce their autonomy over their production, rather it had the opposite effect. As mentioned in the previous chapter, workers in this workshop mainly produced special tools for a specific processing procedure which were required by certain other workshops. Usually, these unconventional tools were new to both the designer and the producer. Those workers therefore often had to make suggestions to revise the nature of raw materials, the machine conditions, and any other technical details related to production. In other words, given that the workers had better knowledge of the operational aspects of production, the novelty of these tools entitled them to a greater right to question the original design. It was this right of questioning that gave them the autonomy over their pace of work, whereby they were able to attribute the causes of delay to other parties, as long as they could provide some seemingly justifiable reasons. The quarrel between Lan Qingshan—a worker in the Instrument Production Workshop—and the tool's designer, which was described in detail in the previous chapter, is a typical example of the workers' autonomy in production.

The Heat Treatment Workshop represented a different example of the workers' exploitation of their autonomy. In contrast to other workshops, workers here worked not individually but in groups. This particular form of production organization was determined by the nature of the work in this shop. Unlike other shops, such as those processing parts or producing tools, the main task of this shop was to move a large number of parts at a time, usually measured in tons, to the furnace for heat treatment according to a predetermined sequence. Unlike the work of other workshops, it took the entire team to get the task done. As a group of workers together moved the heavy parts, it was hard to tell who worked harder and who shirked. Within a team, however, each worker was credited with the arithmetical average of the total work completed. Teamwork combined with egalitarian distribution of credits inevitably bred free-riding behavior, which was in fact an indirect but intentional exploitation of the autonomy through the workers' manipulation of the formal institutions. The uniqueness of production organization in the Heat Treatment Workshop was summarized by the leader of the planning group in this shop:

> We were not individually working in the shop, but working as a team. Each team consisted of six or seven member workers, some of whom assumed the main role, shouldering more work, while others – usually women workers – assisted. Due to the need for teamwork, the production task, which was measured by the required working hours, was calculated for the team, rather than for the individual. Within the team, the working hours were credited equally to member workers. Every morning before work started, a brief meeting would be held (*banqianhui*), at which I assigned a specific part of the day's work to each group leader. Of course, in our workshop, the women workers were usually in an advantageous position in team, because they worked less but received the same.[11]

In a word, regardless of the workshop, the form of production organization, and the kind of work, the rank-and-file workers were all able to seek their autonomy over their daily pace of production without explicitly challenging the formal institutions. Working in these circumstances, the group leaders never enjoyed full-fledged authority and had to work under the constraints of their members' potential "weapons" in the process of production.

Is there any difference between transferred workers, demobilized soldiers, and the Returned Educated Youths in their autonomy over production? To an extent, the differences between these groups could be seen as differences between different workshops. As discussed in the previous chapter, workers' job opportunities were associated with their group belongings. Transferred workers, who were more highly skilled than the other two groups, occupied positions in the Instrument Production Workshop, while demobilized soldiers and the Returned Educated Youths mainly occupied the Heat Treatment Workshop and the Machining Workshop. In fact, the way in which a worker could gain his/her autonomy over production was largely affected by the nature and demand of the work of a particular workshop. Therefore, due to the fact that the assignment of jobs in Jinjiang Factory was closely associated with the workers' origins, the overlapping of inter-group differences with the differences between workshops was by and large a coincidence.

5.4   Conclusion

In view of the discussion above, the toleration of group leaders was also an accommodation derived from their own preference and the capacity of the workshop. The job immobility in the factory meant that they cared more about their reputations and friendships with others. In addition, the job immobility also enabled the workers to develop a series of ways to control their daily pace of work. Underpinned by permanent employment status, these autonomies provided the workers with influential leverage over their relations with the group leaders. In a word, working in these circumstances, the group leaders were not completely willing and able to control strictly.

To some extent, the group leaders' tolerance indicated the importance of the intra-group stability in the factory. Some may argue that the intra-group stability was highly valued because the top priority of factory managers at that time was social stability rather than marginal profitability. This was indeed a factor in the Third Line Enterprises as well. However, this argument ignores the fact that, although marginal profitability was not the pursuit of the factory, the scheduled production plan was the task that managers at all levels had to complete. In these managers' eyes, to fulfill the scheduled production plan and complete the required basic production task might be no less important than the maintenance of intra-group stability, simply because the former was directly related to their individual income. As a result, the concern for stability itself may not be able to fully explain the group leaders' tolerant attitude. Instead, as discussed above, tolerance was a response by managers to the context they were in.

The story of Jinjiang Factory also showed that "managerial dilemma" (Miller 1992) had existed widely in Chinese socialist Enterprises because the behavior of group leaders was conditioned not only by the macro-structure in which they were situated but also by the micro-circumstances coming from the mundane daily life they were embedded in. After all, their member workers were not merely *passive recipients* of the formal institutions but *active agents* who were able to accommodate and even, in a way, change the existing constraints by their understanding and manipulation of state policy, social relations, and working experiences. In this sense, the central problem for managers under socialism was not fundamentally different from that under capitalism. That is, "not to wrest knowledge of the production process from the worker but to persuade workers to co-operate in their own exploitation" (Edwards 1986, p. 46). In the course of "manufacturing consent" (Burawoy 1979), therefore, the role of group leaders at Jinjiang Factory was not only to control but also to adapt and accommodate.

NOTES

1. "Due to local electricity shortages, factories in certain areas usually had their 'weekend' days in turn. That is why the factory had its own unique weekly calendar." Explanation by interviewee Ni Tongzheng.
2. Interview with Liu Chengmin.
3. Interview with Zhu Guiqin.
4. This internal cooperation of working groups should be viewed with caution. Burawoy (1979) recognized the positive effect of immobility within a firm on the development of cooperation among workers. By studying American companies, he argued that "the greater the mobility between jobs, the less opportunity there is to develop the necessary relationship of trust that would counteract tension and competition between workers". In Burawoy's opinion, however, it might be necessary to further clarify that the trusting relationship in the working group might not necessarily be related to altruistic values. The trust between group leaders and their workers, instead, might be more appropriately understood as them sharing the common knowledge that one side is currently cooperating and will do so as long as it appears that the other side will.
5. Interview with Fu Qianwei.
6. Interview with Cao Mingshen.
7. Interview with Chen Youbai.
8. Interview with Fu Jinhai.
9. Interview with Gu Jiwei.
10. Interview with Gu Jiwei.
11. Interview with Chen Mingzhen.

REFERENCES

Axelrod, Robert. 1984. *The Evolution of Cooperation*, New York: Basic Books.
Burawoy, Michael. 1979. *Manufacturing Consent: Changes in the Labor Process Under Monopoly Capitalism*, Chicago: University of Chicago Press.
Chen, Feng. 2003 (April). Industrial Restructuring and Workers' Resistance in China, *Modern China*, 29 (2):237–62.
Chen, Calvin. 2006. Work, Conformity, and Defiance: Strategies of Resistance and Control in China's Township and Village Enterprises, in Eyferth, Jacob, ed.

How China Works: Perspectives on the Twentieth-Century Industrial Workplace, London and New York: Routledge.

Cai, Yongshun. 2006. *State and Laid-Off Workers in Reform China: The Silent and Collective Action of the Retrenched*, London: Routledge.

Edwards, P. K. 1986. *Conflict at Work: A Materialist Analysis of Workplace Relations*, Oxford: Basil Blackwell.

Gold, Thomas B. 1980 (December). Back to the City: The Return of Shanghai's Educated Youth, *The China Quarterly*, 84:755–70.

Hurst, William. 2009. *The Chinese Worker After Socialism*, Cambridge: Cambridge University Press.

Lu, Feng, 1989. Danwei: A Unique Form of Social Organization, *Chinese Social Science*, 1:71–88.

Li, Hanlin. 1993. China's Danwei Phenomenon and the Mechanisms of Conformity in Urban Communities, *Sociology Research*, 5:23–32.

Liu, Jianjun. 2002. *The Danwei China: Individual, Organization and the State in the System of Social Control*, Tianjin: Tianjin People's Publishing House.

Lee, Ching Kwan. 2007. *Against the Law: Labor Protest in China's Rustbelt and Sunbelt*, Berkeley: University of Los Angeles.

McLaren, Anne. 1979 (July). The Educated Youth Return: The Poster Campaign in Shanghai from November 1978 to March 1979, *The Australian Journal of Chinese Affairs*, 2:1–20.

Miller, J. Gary. 1992. *Managerial Dilemmas: The Political Economy of Hierarchy*, New York: Cambridge University Press.

Perry, Elizabeth. 1994 (March). Shanghai's Strike Wave of 1957, *The China Quarterly*, 137:1–27.

Walder, Andrew G. 1986. *Communist Neo-Traditionalism: Work and Authority in Chinese Industry*, Berkeley: University of California Press.

Womack, Brantly. 1991 (June). Transfigured Community: Neo-Traditionalism and Work Unit Socialism in China, *The China Quarterly*, 126:313–332.

Zhao, Minghua and Theo Nichols. 1996 (July). Management Control of Labor in State-Owned Enterprises: Cases from the Textile Industry, *The China Journal*, 36:1–21.

CHAPTER 6

Toleration in Practice (1): The Phenomenon of Absenteeism

During the late 1970s and the 1980s, persistent and rampant absenteeism had been a serious problem for Jinjiang Factory's management. It was a problem not only in one or two workshops but in the whole factory. I choose the issue of absenteeism as an example to show the tolerating strategy for two reasons. First, it is perhaps the most common problem that management needs to deal with in the day-to-day routine. As Edwards and Whitston say, "the problem of persuading workers to attend work regularly is as old as capitalism" (Edwards and Whitston 1993, p. 5). Second, and more importantly, it is intrinsically linked to order in the workplace. Numerous critiques have argued that absenteeism is not merely a reflection of inadequate career satisfaction of individual employees. Rather, as part of a conflict-laden relationship between employers and workers (Edwards and Scullion 1985), it is closely related to its organizational setting (Marcus and Smith 1985) and has very different social meanings (Johns and Nicholson 1982). Absenteeism is thus a window through which the wider issue of order and relationships in the workplace can be understood.

In this study "absence" means a state of being away from duty without the factory's permission. "Absenteeism" refers to the habitual pattern of this state. Usually, the absenteeism carries connotations of the conscious *violation* of formal factory rules, but it does not necessarily refer to the workers' deliberate *defiance* or non-overt *resistance*. What distinguishes the former from the latter is the action's potential purpose toward the status quo. An action that is a simple violation of the rules, though it

© The Author(s) 2018
C. Chen, *Toleration*, New Perspectives on Chinese Politics and
Society, https://doi.org/10.1007/978-981-10-8941-1_6

occurs consciously, does not necessarily represent the desire of workers to change existing circumstances. It occurs only because of certain individual needs, such as housework, family illness, and so on. In contrast, a resisting action usually expresses the workers' dissatisfaction with the status quo and their desire for change. In Jinjiang Factory, workers' absenteeism takes many different forms. It includes not only the most common cases of arriving late and leaving early but also many more covert behaviors that are effectively the equivalent of physical absence, such as false sick leave, chatting, or carrying on personal business during working hours, deliberately slowing down the pace of toilet visits, collecting water, and so on.

This chapter aims to present an overview of absenteeism in Jinjiang Factory in two sections. The first section illustrates the severity of the factory's absenteeism in a quantitative way. In the second section, I briefly describe two categories of situation leading to workers' absences: misbehavior in work and periodic and impromptu personal matters.

6.1   Discussion of Absenteeism in Conferences

Conferences play an indispensable role in the factory's management process. They deliver instructions from above, collect information from the grass roots, and absorb useful opinions from all sides. As a result, what is discussed in the conferences, by and large, is a mirror of what is happening in the factory. Following this logic, this section uses the proportion of conferences that discussed absenteeism to indicate the degree of absenteeism in general. Using this indicator has at least three advantages. First, it reflects the absenteeism problem in the whole factory rather than in one or two workshops. Second, since the factory's conferences are scheduled to a routine, with only a few exceptions, the proportion can be compared across years. Third, though it fails to present the precise number of absences, it can properly capture the general picture of the factory's absenteeism problem. This is simply because the factory's managers govern by relying not only on paper records of absences, but also on their understanding of what is actually happening in practice. In fact, due to the group leader's multifarious tricks, which will be discussed in detail in Chap. 7, the paper absence records are not in fact as precise as expected.

Conferences at Jinjiang Factory could be classified into four types. The meeting of party branch secretaries was one of the most important conferences. It was a scheduled monthly discussion focusing mainly on ideological education, new party member recruitment, and so on. The secretary of the factory's party committee chaired the meeting. Production issues were discussed at a meeting of the factory's middle-level cadres. This was also a scheduled monthly meeting, attended by workshop directors and heads of the factory's functional departments. The factory director was in charge of this meeting.

Assessment meetings were also scheduled on a monthly basis. Here the factory's economic planning department would release its assessment of the work of every workshop and functional department. Monthly bonuses were allocated on the basis of this report. The production-scheduling meeting (*shengchan diaoduhui*) was the fourth type of factory conference. It took place twice every week, once on Friday afternoon, called the "primary scheduling meeting" (*yiji diaoduhui*), and once on Tuesday afternoon, called the "secondary scheduling meeting" (*erji diaoduhui*). At the primary scheduling meeting, all the factory's functional departments, such as the quality control department or even the security department, were represented, while, at the secondary scheduling meeting, the production plan was delivered and coordinated across sections of the various workshops.

The fixed frequency of all these conferences, excluding public holidays, meant that there were 132 factory conferences a year. The total number of conferences (of all four types) at which absenteeism was mentioned was calculated from the meeting minutes. Thanks to Jinjiang Factory's Office of Retirement Services, many of these minutes were saved upon the factory's bankruptcy. The earliest dates from 1978. In these minutes, it is worth noting that not all conferences that mention absenteeism should be included in the calculation. For example, in some meetings, it was mentioned only to note a relative decrease in worker absence rather than an increase. After eliminating such discussions, the proportion over the period 1978–1989 was calculated and the results are shown in Fig. 6.1.

As can be seen, during this period, the proportion of conferences mentioning absenteeism was consistently higher than 0.5 (50%) and peaked at 0.79 (79%) in 1981. As a result, it can be speculated that absenteeism in Jinjiang Factory had been so serious that it could not be treated lightly in the routine work. A noticeable change took place in 1982, when the proportion fell sharply to 0.62, and this downward trend continued until 1984. This change was probably due to the institution of new rules; in 1982, the factory enacted a new regulation aimed at reducing workers' absences. This regulation decreed that anyone who needed to leave work for less than two hours must apply for an exit pass, noting the exact leaving

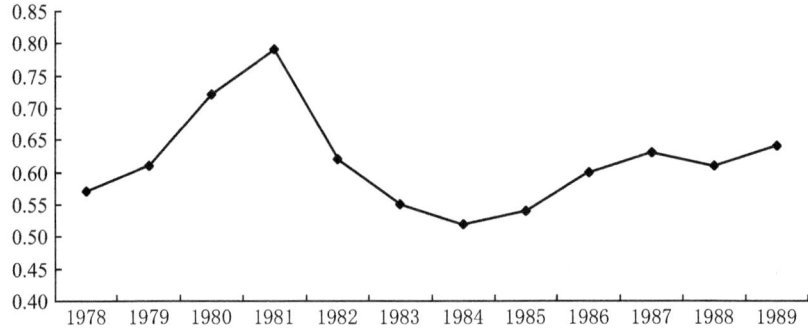

Fig. 6.1 Proportion of conferences where absenteeism was mentioned (1978–1989)

and returning time. Subsequently, in 1983, the factory implemented the "Factory Rules and Regulations for Workers and Staff Members" (*changgui changji zhigong shouze*), further linking individual performance to the economic interest. However, these new rules and regulations were not effective for long. As is shown in Fig. 6.1, the proportion returns to a slight increase between 1985 and 1989.

Though the indicator used in this section is not ideal, it indirectly shows the wide spread existence of absenteeism through a quantitative method. Why were workers in the Jinjiang Factory going absent? What excuses did they usually use to ask for leave? These questions are the focus of the following section.

6.2   Absenteeism in Practice

In general, workers' absenteeism in Jinjiang Factory refers to all illicit behavior in attempts to shirk duties and seek personal free time. Absence occurs due to either misbehavior in the workshop or personal matters. Absenteeism in Jinjiang Factory was by no means a rare or sporadic problem. Rather, it was widespread and frequent.

Absence Due to Misbehaviors

A variety of misbehaviors occurred in the workshop. Non-work activity during working hours was perhaps the most surreptitious form of absence—workers fulfilled their private needs without leaving their seats.

A typical example would be female workers knitting during working hours. This phenomenon was especially common among those performing less-demanding jobs. As long as they were able to meet their quantitative target at the last minute, devoting some time to private affairs seemed acceptable in their eyes.

> As far as I know, some women workers always knitted during working time. This was especially the case for workers whose job was light and easy. I had a colleague who used to work in the Instrument Production Workshop and later transferred to the factory warehouse. In the warehouse, her daily work was just to distribute materials and instruments to different workshops. She needed to do nothing heavy and difficult. So she spent most of her time on knitting sweaters for her husband and child.[1]

Male workers did not do such handicrafts, but they had their own way to kill time. Whenever they felt tired or bored with their work, they wandered around their workshop with a cup of tea, approaching some of their workmates to share news, gossip, and, rumors.

> Workers always liked to *chuiniupi* (chat)[2] with their colleagues. Yes, indeed, sometimes they just wandered in the workshop and looked here and there. You may think this was not a big deal. In fact, however, it was serious because it not only delayed the progress of the wanderer's own work, but also affected others' work. The water room where they fetched boiled water was their favorite place to get together. Everyone just stood in the room, holding their tea cup, talking, laughing and not in a hurry to get back to their work.[3]

The habit of *chuiniupi* among workers was not unique to Cao Mingshen's workshop; rather it was widespread throughout the factory, reducing the whole factory's efficiency. The seriousness of this problem can be seen from Tan Yi's meeting minutes, which recorded the factory's determination to counter *chuiniupi* with a series of specific measures:

> October 16, 1983. Meeting of the Party Branch Secretaries
>   The illicit behavior not only includes arriving late, leaving early, or sneaking away. It also includes the following: *chuiniupi*, turning on the machine but not working, and wandering around in the workshop. The factory should establish disciplinary inspection groups on three levels. At the factory level, the deputy director in charge of human resources will be the group

leader; at the workshop level, the deputy director of the workshop will be the group leader; and in the production group, the group leaders will take the responsibility. Anyone who is caught for the first time will be recorded and educated by the relevant leader; if caught for a second time, the offender will have to submit a written report; fines will apply for a third occasion. In addition, performance points of every relevant workshop will be deducted regardless of the reason for the breach.

Taking a shower during working hours was another form of misbehavior causing absence. Besides the factory shower room, the Heat Treatment Workshop was another place where workers could take showers. Unlike the factory's shower room, which had fixed opening hours, hot water would be available as soon as the workshop was in operation. As a result, workers could take a shower at any time during the day.

Workers worked in the factory as if they were at home. They had a weak sense of discipline. For example, many workers would come to my [hot treatment] workshop for a shower in the afternoon during working time. They usually came with their friends. Some female workers even took their children for a shower. For a period of time, can you imagine, my main job, as a secretary of the party branch of the workshop, was to sit in front of the gate and stop them from entering the bathroom. I remember once I heard someone showering when I passed by. I went in and forcibly chased them out. They nearly fought with me. Both the factory and the workshop did make some regulations [to tackle] this behavior, but it seems very difficult to eradicate this problem.[4]

Indeed, this problem persisted and frustrated the management for a long time, appearing in Tan Yi's meeting minutes and working diary several times over the years.

July 5, 1982. Meeting of Party Branch Secretaries

Workers were not allowed to take a shower before 3 pm.

...

March 10, 1984. Meeting of the Workshop Disciplinary Inspection Group

Regulations on showering: workers were not allowed to take a shower before 2:30 pm. Also, parents were not allowed to take their children for a shower during working time.

...

May 17, 1987 Sunday (Sunny)

This afternoon, Zhang Ming brought his classmates to the workshop for a shower before the approved time. I took him to the office and asked him to learn the factory regulations carefully.

Absence for Personal Matters

Personal matters were another cause of workers' absenteeism. This refers to both common personal issues and ad hoc ones. Generally speaking, these various personal issues arose because of two broad facts in Jinjiang Factory—the heterogeneous component of workers on the one hand and the isolated living conditions on the other.

A typical example of common personal matters was the farm work of the demobilized soldiers. Unlike the Returned Educated Youths and transferred workers, the demobilized soldiers played a dual role. They were workers in the industrial enterprises and, at the same time, peasants responsible for their family's farm work. Every year during the peak seasons in spring and autumn, they usually had to ask for leave for at least half a month. No matter how crucial the production task was, this personal business had to be accepted as a reason for leave because, in these workers' eyes, the crops at home were far more important than receiving a performance bonus for the same month.

The demobilized soldiers were not the only group that had reasonable excuses; the transferred workers also had their own versions. Since they had been transferred from the east to the far away west, they had very few opportunities to go home for visits due to the limited number of days designated for annual home leave as well as the high cost of transportation. As a result, whenever they had a chance of home leave, they were desperate to extend the period as much as possible. As one transferred worker from Shanghai recalled, "I could only have 15 days for my trip home, but I fabricated a reason to be granted more days. I reported that I also needed to take a study tour in a model factory in Shanghai. Eventually, I got another three days as business leave."[5]

Ad hoc matters also led to workers' absences. The high frequency of such instances was partially due to the workers' unique working conditions. In the isolated mountain area, despite the existence of periodic markets in nearby towns, workers in Jinjiang Factory made full use of empty land within their resident sites, planting many different vegetables, such as garlic, spring onion, potato, and tomato. Some even fed chickens there. As recorded in Tan Yi's conference notes, "(October 13, 1983, Meeting of

Personnel Managers) As long as the chickens do not crow, feeding could be allowed." Even though these planting and feeding activities were very limited and usually on a tiny scale, they occurred frequently enough to distract some workers from their industrial work occasionally.

The Province of Sichuan is situated in the great Sichuan basin. Besieged by winding high mountains, it is subject to a lot of rain from June to September. In this period, Sichuan's weather is also very unpredictable. It is very common to have bright sunshine in the morning and heavy rain in the afternoon. On some days during this period, it rains two or even three times a day. Whenever the workers spotted any hint of rain, they usually rushed home for some pre-emptive work.

Crops were not the only things that needed to be protected against the heavy downpours. Living in the humid Sichuan basin, people usually aired their quilts and clothes on balconies or on the bushes around the dormitories whenever it was sunny. In the event of a sudden change of weather, they had to ask for leave to bring back their belongings hanging outside as quickly as possible.

These changeable climatic conditions caused a lot of problems in the workers' lives and the factory's production. But to the workers, the silver lining was that it was a reasonable excuse to ask for a short leave, from which they might never return. Given the proximity of the factory and workers' dormitories, it might not be fair to argue that the weather was an absurd excuse and should be forbidden completely. The vice deputy director of the factory explained their considerations:

> You may think that to approve their leave for changeable weather is weird or even ridiculous, but we had to take into consideration the reality. In this factory—and actually I think it may be similar in many Third Line factories—the production site was very close to the residential site. Workers would not spend too much time getting home. So if they knew that the weather was about to change, it was very natural that they wanted to bring their quilts and clothes back home. The changeable weather is one reality; the short distance between home and workshop is also a reality in this factory. So if you just forbade them from moving their quilts and clothes and let them be soaked, it appeared very unreasonable (*bujiangli*). After all, the decision should be made on a case-by-case basis (*juti wenti juti fenxi*).[6]

Yu Xuehui's comments illustrate that workers' sudden leave to get back to the airing quilts should be understood because of the changeable weather in Sichuan and, more importantly, the close proximity of their residential site and working place. In other words, in this case, the special spatial features of Jinjiang Factory had redrawn the boundary of acceptability of sudden leave.

6.3   Conclusion

This chapter introduces the problem of absenteeism in Jinjiang Factory from two aspects—the seriousness of absenteeism and the factors that led to the workers' absences. Using the factory's meeting minutes, I show that during the late 1970s and the 1980s, the problem of absenteeism was a phenomenon existing throughout the whole factory rather than only one or two workshops. Workers' misbehavior in working time and periodic impromptu personal matters were two main types of factors leading to workers' absences.

In the sociological literature on absence, the question of gender has attracted scholars' attention. According to this strand of literature, the factors taken as reasons for absence differ between men and women. Specifically, the "non-work pressures to go absent are likely to be greater on women than on men" (Edwards and Whitston 1989, p. 10). As Pollert (1981) comments, "absence can be genuine escape for men whereas for women it may mean confronting a pile of work at home". Haccoun and Dupont's (1988) work also offers some confirmation: women are more likely to spend a day's absence on "obligatory activities" such as housework. On this point, the present work seems no different from these previous studies. Among the abovementioned factors, knitting, babysitting, taking care of airing quilts, and so on, were the usual reasons for female workers' absences, while drunkenness, farm work, and so on were the reasons leading to male workers' absences. Some reasons were also used by both female and male workers, such as showering at work and going home for visits. In sum, at Jinjiang Factory, gender might not cause any numerical difference between female and male workers' absences, but it was indeed a variable related to the different reasons for absences.

In the face of workers' absenteeism, how did the grass-roots group leaders organize their production in a tolerating way? I will answer this question in the following chapter.

NOTES

1. Interview with Zhu Guiqin.
2. *Chuiniupi* is a dialectic expression in Sichuan province which can be translated literally as "boast". However, when used by a local of Sichuan, it does not refer to the annoying behavior that the word "boast" really indicates. It actually means chatting with others.
3. Interview with Cao Mingsheng.
4. Interview with Tan Yi.
5. Interview with Zhu Guiqin.
6. Interview with Yu Xuehui.

REFERENCES

Edwards, Paul and Collin Whitston. 1989 (March). Industrial Discipline, the Control of Attendance and the Subordination of Labor: Towards an Integrated Analysis, *Work, Employment and Society*, 3:1–28.

Edwards, Paul and Collin Whitston. 1993. *Attending to Work: The Management of Attendance and Shopfloor Order*, Oxford: Blackwell.

Edwards, Paul and Hugh Scullion. 1985 (August). Absenteeism and the Control of Work, *Sociological Review*, 32:547–72.

Haccoun, R. and S. Dupont. 1988. Une analyse des comportements de travailleurs masculins et feminins selon deux formes d'absence au travail, *Relations Industrielles*, 43 (1): 153–65. Cited from Edwards, Paul and Collin Whitston. 1989 (March). Industrial Discipline, the Control of Attendance and the Subordination of Labor: Towards an Integrated Analysis, *Work, Employment and Society*, 3:1–28.

Johns, Gary and Nigel Nicholson. 1982. The Meaning of Absence, in Staw, B. M. and L. L. Cummings, eds. *Research in Organizational Behavior*, Vol. 4, Greenwich, Conn: JAI.

Marcus, Philip M. and Catherine B. Smith. 1985 (August). Absenteeism in an Organizational Context, *Work and Occupations*, 12:251–68.

Pollert, Anna. 1981. *Girls, Wives, Factory Lives*, London: Macmillan.

CHAPTER 7

Toleration in Practice (2): The Governance of Absenteeism

The workshop was a battlefield. Whether you could win the war depended on your own talents. You needed to know how to unite this disparate group of individuals (sanjiao jiuliu)
Fu Jinhai, December 22, 2013

In the analysis of Chinese industrial relations, very few studies make the effort to investigate governance at the group level. Instead, the existing literature is more interested in the politics at more macro levels, such as the factory level, tackling questions such as how a factory disciplines its workers and how the relationship between businesses and governments affects conflicts and cooperation in the workshop. In these works, governance within groups is taken as a reflection of the factory's governing system, and the role of group leader is simply that of a policy implementer whose interests are convergent with those of his senior bosses. However, group governance is not as simple as these previous studies assumed. As the interviewee Fu Jinhai, the camshaft group leader in the Machining Workshop, said, the workshop was a battlefield and you had to know how to deal with different kinds of people.

Among the scholars studying the governance of small production groups, Walder made perhaps the most significant contribution by highlighting the powerful role of the group leaders. According to him, group leaders were pivotal in the evaluation of workers' pay rises and promotions, granting travel permissions and approving requests for personal leave, paid vacations, home leave, travel supplements, housing assignments, extra ration coupons, loans, and relief payments (Walder 1986, p. 104). Granting (or not) these necessities of life constituted the carrots and sticks by which the group leaders controlled and mobilized their member workers through the construction of a patron–client relationship with the activists who helped in the control in exchange for preferential treatment by their leaders. Walder refers to this system of control in China's socialist factories as "principled particularism".

However, Zhou contends against Walder by pointing out that, before the reform of SOEs, the workers' basic necessities had in fact been institutionally guaranteed. Therefore, given that the resources controlled by the lower managers were not as great as Walder claimed, the patron–client relationship might not be very effective (Zhou 1999). By taking the potential strength of "the weak" into account, Womack (1991) echoed Zhou and argued that Walder's "over-concentration on state power overlooks the concrete limits on leadership discretion, ignores the informality of power in small-scale, stable situations, and produces a skewed and unrealistic view of workplace interrelationships".

Zhou and Womack's criticism suggests that the leaders were not as powerful as they appeared and, for that matter, the workers were by no means powerless either. At this point, the constant absenteeism in Jinjiang Factory provides some evidence to this effect. This power parity between the group leaders and their workers makes the group governance seem more puzzling. If workers had their own way of resisting, then how did group leaders maintain production in the face of constant interruptions? In this chapter, I show that rather than strictly enacting the regulations, group leaders in Jinjiang Factory gave their toleration to workers' absences. This benign and tolerating strategy was based on three building blocks: the reinterpretation of the absenteeism, the multi-actors' exchange, and the tactics sustaining the exchange. It is worth noting that the focus on toleration is not meant to deny or replace Walder's concept of principled particularism. Rather, it is intended to provide an alternative governance mechanism which is more likely and perhaps was more effective in factories like Jinjiang, which was isolated from the outside world but had many complex internal social interconnections.

This chapter includes two broad sections. The first illustrates the concept, operating mechanism, and basic features of toleration. The second introduces the normal tactics that underpin the tolerating governance.

7.1   Reinterpretation of Absenteeism: The Exceptional Circumstances

In Jinjiang Factory, absenteeism was usually reinterpreted as the exceptional circumstances. This reinterpretation was derived from a consensus that everyone was unique in some way and unexceptionally had his/her exceptional circumstances in day-to-day working experiences, which should be considered as reasonable excuses for absence in daily interactions.[1] Therefore, this understanding was exceptional because it recognized individual uniqueness, while it was also *un*exceptional because it emphasized the equity of uniquenesses among individuals. According to this understanding and reinterpretation, the multifarious reasons causing workers' absences were in a way justifiable. It can be seen that this informal principle was philosophically in contrast with the formal institutions of the factory. If the formal institutions can be understood as a set of rules enacted to bring about the same behavior under the same standard, the reinterpretation is a consensus on a purely case-by-case basis. The essence of the former is "de-differentiation", while the latter is to reintroduce the differences between workers.

Tolerance of workers' absences was certain to delay the production of the group to some degree. To cover the absentees' production tasks, group leaders had to seek help from other workers. In this process, a multi-actors' exchange occurred between the absent workers, other member workers, and the group leader. As the workers took turns to be absent, this exchange circulated constantly among members who were to cover and be covered by one another. As a result, though production was constantly interrupted by the workers' numerous absences, group leaders were able to maintain their productions.

7.2   Exchange Among Multiple Actors

In the event of a worker's absence, the multi-actors' exchange took place between the absent worker, the member colleagues, and their group leader. In this exchange, the absent worker was the "taker", gaining tolerance and assistance from his/her leader and member colleagues, while the member colleagues were the "donor", giving their assistance to both their leader and the absent worker. The group leader therefore usually acted as a coordinator, who gave to and took from the other two parties simultaneously.

The most simplified equilibrium of the multi-actors exchange is represented in Fig. 7.1.

Figure 7.1 represents a typical reciprocal exchange. According to the classic literature on social networks, reciprocity takes place as the favor is returned to the same person who donates the help (Wasserman and Faust 1994). In fact, however, this kind of reciprocity rarely occurred, because the workers' absent behaviors happened in a very random way. As a result, the tolerance and assistance were not exchanged between group members in a typically reciprocal fashion, but in a form that I call "favor-pooling". This involves two types of exchange, which were introduced by Ekeh (1974): the "chain generalized exchange" and the "individual-focused net generalized exchange". A common feature of these two types of exchange is that the favor will be returned by offering help and assistance to a different member in the future.

Figure 7.2 displays the equilibrium of the "chain generalized exchange". In this exchange, everyone indirectly gives back to those who provided

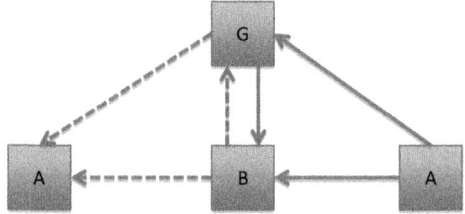

Fig. 7.1 Simplified equilibrium of the exchange among multiple actors. (Note: In the exchange identified by the solid arrows, B is the absent worker and A is the donor of assistance, while in the exchange identified by the dotted arrows, the give-and-take relations are reversed. "G" refers to the coordinating group leader and "→" denotes "gives to")

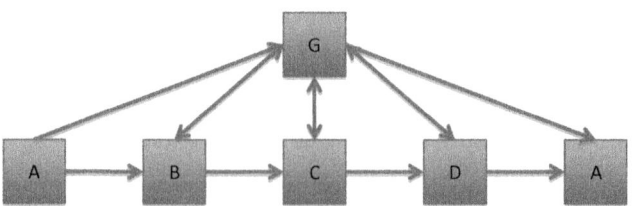

Fig. 7.2 Equilibrium of the chain generalized exchange

help. In other words, even though the donating worker may not be able to receive help from the taker directly, he/she will be repaid by others in the future. As a result, this equilibrium is not achieved in every exchange, but it is maintained and perpetuated with continuous exchanges going on between all group members as a whole. As the interviewee Fu Jinhai reported:

> Living in this isolated place, we could not count on others but only ourselves. As a result, you had to be thoughtful about personal matters. Saving the airing quilt, moving house, extending leave for farm work or visiting relatives, looking after the sick fellows and so on, all these were justifiable exceptional circumstances. This was our actual condition. Therefore, what our group leaders could do was to coordinate our production work among members. This time, you helped me; next time, I helped others. Some of the help was directly mutual, while others were not, but we did not care too much because we knew we would need and receive the help some day from someone.[2]

Figure 7.3 illustrates the equilibrium of the individual-focused net generalized exchange. Here, the donor is not a single person, but a collection of individuals. This type of exchange was not unusual in Jinjiang Factory either. One typical example is the assistance rendered to demobilized soldiers for farm work at their family homes. As mentioned earlier, demobilized soldiers accounted for almost one-third of the factory's workforce. They were also the main force in front production lines. Many of these workers' homes were located in nearby counties. Every spring and autumn, they needed to go home to work on the family farm. In order to shorten their leave and minimize production delays, the group leaders motivated some other member workers to help them with farming or production work.

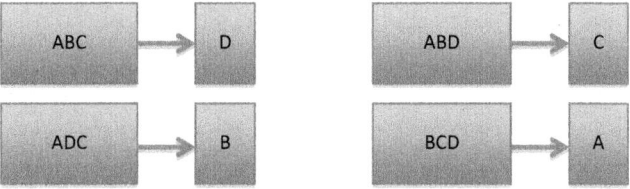

Fig. 7.3 Equilibrium of the individual-focused net generalized exchange

A second example of this exchange can be seen when moving house. As Tan Yi recalled in Chap. 3, every worker at Jinjiang Factory would move house several times: from a dormitory to a small apartment, then to a medium-sized apartment, and later to a medium-large apartment. Some leaders might even have to move once again, from the medium-large to a large apartment. Every time a worker needed to move house, the group leader would assign some other member workers to provide help. For some families with too much furniture, they even borrowed the factory's trucks to help those moving.

The enforcement of these exchanges required the consent of donors. Put differently, why would member colleagues agree to donate their help? This can be understood from three perspectives. First, the production group was not big and workers knew each other very well; some of them were even friends or relatives. The small group and well-acquainted relationships within it helped to reduce the "free rider" problem and made members more accountable to each other. Second, as mentioned earlier, workers at Jinjiang Factory were isolated from the outside world and placed in a relatively fixed job niche. In this context, interactions among members can be regarded as repeated games, in which players played a strategy of "tit-for-tat". In these games, as predicted by game theory, playing the cooperative strategy is feasible at equilibrium because, in the long run, the benefits of cooperation can exceed the gains from cheating. Third, the cooperative attitude was also maintained by group leaders' power of surveillance and punishment, as interviewees Fu Jinhai, Fang Mingqi, and Chen Mingzhen all reported:

> If someone refused my request, I would warn him/her that "if you refuse, you will not gain any help from me in the future!" As a group leader, we more or less controlled some resources they needed and they had to consider their decisions carefully.[3]

Thus far, I have clarified the content and operating mechanism of the tolerating strategy in control of absenteeism. Four features of this unique governing system stand out from the analysis, on which I now elaborate.

7.3   CHARACTERISTICS OF MULTI-ACTORS EXCHANGE

The first feature is that it involved matters outside one's *de jure* duties (*fenwai shi*), or sometimes even matters that violated the factory's regulations. Helping demobilized-soldier workers with their farm work, tolerance of drunkenness during working hours, trading working hours within the group, building up the group's private coffer, falsifying overtime hours, privately extending members' holiday leave, and so on were all visible favors that could be exchanged in the group. In this process, the factory's regulations and discipline implicitly functioned as a benchmark used to gauge the value of an exchanged favor. The more the favor violated the regulations, the higher its value and the closer the relationship between both sides. In other words, the group's internal "loyalty" was displayed and preserved by the "betrayal" toward outsiders. This feature of the exchange distinguishes it from the principled particularism argued by Walder. According to him, "principled particularism is a mixed type: it has the structural attributes of a vertical patron–client tie, but the content of the tie is the impersonal one prescribed by the ideological orientation" (Walder 1986, p. 132). By contrast, the favor exchange based on the consideration of exceptional circumstances is entirely personal. This occurred because personal exceptionalism was exchanged for personal necessity, and the parties involved in the exchange ended up in a closer personal relationship.

The unique content of the exchange gives rise to its second feature. The driver for an exchange was not purely rational and value-equivalent; it also included many irrational elements. Since the favor was usually something forbidden by the regulations, it was taken by the recipient as an extra consideration (*ewai zhaogu*), exclusively given by the donor. In addition, as the substance of the favor was in fact illegal, it not only embodied the donor's initiative but also required some sort of personal sacrifice on the part of the donor, who bore the risk of being punished. In these circumstances, the calculable portion of the debt was no longer as essential as it would be in a pure market exchange, while the feeling of gratitude played a greater role in the flow of interactions. With the feeling of gratitude, the recipient's repayment need not be equivalent to what he/she received in value, but the recipient must demonstrate his/her eagerness to pay back. For example, if a demobilized soldier received help for his family's farm work from colleagues who were Returned Educated Youths or transferred workers, there was no way for him to return the favor by providing the same help (farming), but he could return the favor by assisting his colleagues with moving house, covering their production work when they were sick or drunk, and so on. In this regard, the favor exchange was not the equilibrium of value but the equilibrium of interaction. As illustrated in Figs. 19 and 20, equilibrium is not achieved in every single exchange;

rather it is embodied in a stream of gives and takes whose value was difficult to calculate. Therefore, every single exchange of favors was not completely unique and independent. Instead, it usually had a long-lasting effect on both sides by accumulating their sense of cooperation, strengthening their confidence of trust, and so on. In addition, even the favor given in the name of exceptional circumstances was not completely out of the donor's rationality. As many interviewees repeated, "Life could never be uphill all the time; it was sometimes downhill. When we put ourselves in the shoes of others, many troubles they encountered could and should be understood. After all, while the regulation was rigid, the people were flexible."[4] This statement revealed that the workers' empathy, rather than merely their rationality, also motivated the donation of favors. A by-product of this semi-rational exchange was the development of informal social relations within the group. In extreme cases, it could even give birth to personal loyalty or a sense of brotherhood between the donor and recipient. As one worker in the Machining Workshop said, "He [the group leader] had been really kind and generous to me (*duiwo gouyisi*), and I was willing to give my help whenever he needed it."[5] Of course, not all workers had such positive impressions of their leaders and were so determined to provide help in case of need, but it is hard to deny that the development of different forms of informal relations deepened the irrational elements of favor exchange. In this sense, the exchange among multiple actors is a process of accumulation of "symbolic capital" within the group (Bourdieu 1977). By exchanging incalculable favors, the apparent economic debt is eventually transmuted into a moral-and-affective-like obligation to the leader and the member colleagues.

The irrational aspect of this favor exchange distinguishes it from the previously argued gift economy, also known as the art of *guanxi*. The importance of *guanxi* in Chinese daily life has long been valued by political scientists (Chan and Unger 1982; Solinger 1983; Yang 1989; Bian 1997). In their eyes, *guanxi* is not only the means for receiving material gains but also the end of interactions. Yang (1989) extends the understanding of the role of *guanxi* by arguing that it is the centrality of symbolic interest or capital in the conversion of values that distinguishes it from other forms of exchange. The symbolic interest, according to her, increases as the social investment or the incorporation of personal substance yields "an unbalanced state of indebtedness, gratitude, or obligation on the part of the *guanxi* target, or a moral advantage and superior symbolic status for the donor" (Yang 1989, p. 46). This observation provides an innovative way to understand the working mechanism of *guanxi*, but it was still in the straightjacket of rationalism. Like other scholars, Yang (1989, p. 35) recognizes that the art of *guanxi* was essentially a tactic composed of calculated actions. The ultimate purpose of its use was the pursuit of both diffused social ends and calculated instrumental ends. Therefore, for the donors, giving is intentionally for taking; for the recipients, their repayment, in whatever form, is for the restoration of their lost status or advantage toward the donors. In a word, such an exchange started from and ended with the purely rational calculations of both sides. While it seems naive to claim the total irrationality of the exchange, it is unreasonable to reduce its process to a purely rational one. As discussed above, the exchange among multiple actors was partly based on the workers' empathy. Therefore, for the donors, the decision to provide help— such as covering for sick colleagues or helping demobilized soldiers with farming—comes not only from their individual cost and benefit analysis but also from their understanding and consideration of the exceptional circumstances. For the recipients, they not only repaid the amount they gained from the donor, or merely for their restoration of lost status or advantage but also were affected by a feeling of gratitude. Thus, it can be seen in Jinjiang Factory that the one-time "gift" from the donor could often be repaid several times by the recipient. Moreover, as relations between the two sides become closer and closer as their exchange continues, the irrational aspect appears more and more obvious. It is worth pointing out that the emphasis on the irrational aspect here is not to erase the rational elements entirely from the exchange. Rather, the point is that, without recognizing the irrational substance, it seems impossible to understand the sometimes unequal and incalculable exchanges that continually occurred in the daily activities of the production groups.

The third feature of the exchange between group leaders and member workers was its spillover effect. This can be understood from two perspectives. First, the exchange between the leader and the target worker would extend to other workers in the group. This was simply because sometimes the favor could not be given by the leaders without the assistance of other workers. Helping the demobilized soldiers to do their farm work, buying and selling working hours among members, covering shifts, and so on needed to involve more than one member worker. In these cases, the recipient workers not only owed their leaders for the permission but also owed their colleagues for their direct donation of the favor. Over time, this extended exchange relationship further tightened the connections between member workers; meanwhile, it also helped the leaders guarantee the completion of the group task by balancing the production among workers. Second, one occurrence of the exchange between the leader and a certain target member worker could increase other workers' expectations of similar exchanges happening in the future. The occurrence of the exchange sent out a signal that the leader was probably flexible enough to tolerate some exceptional cases. Thus, they could carry out similar exchanges as and when needed.

The fourth feature of the exchange was that it applied to the member workers relatively equally. In other words, the group leaders' consideration of exceptional circumstances was not a privilege of any particular workers. Farm work was not considered more urgent than taking care of a sick child; occasionally arriving late for work was not necessarily less serious than privately extending holiday leave. Each instance was considered independently and could not be compared with another. Moreover, the members' increased expectation of equal treatment raised the cost of the leaders' unfair behavior. Unequal treatment, once discovered, would challenge the group leaders' authority, as the workers who were unfairly treated would retaliate with a series of "weapons" introduced in the previous section. In some extreme cases, the group leaders could even be removed from power by their members' open resistance. It was in this principle of relative equality that the rational aspect of the toleration lay. This feature also differentiates toleration from Walder's neo-traditionalism. The latter is essentially a differentiating governing system in which activist workers are treated preferentially, while non-activists are at a disadvantage (Walder 1986). By contrast, under group leaders' toleration, all workers are treated on an equal basis. In this sense, compared to the "elitism" argued by Walder, egalitarianism was more popularly employed in governing the production groups in Jinjiang Factory.

In a word, group governance in Jinjiang Factory was conducted through the exchange of consideration of each other's exceptional circumstances. The recognition and acceptance of the exceptional circumstances were irrational to some extent, while the undifferentiated principle was more of a rational choice by the group leaders. A direct consequence of this exchange was the development of informal relationships between group leaders and their member workers. Meanwhile, the connections among the member workers were also strengthened, thanks to the spillover effect of the exchange. Given that the workers' job positions were closely associated with their background, the exchange among multiple actors and the interconnected social networks were tightly interrelated and mutually reinforcing. On the one hand, the exchange helped in developing and reinforcing the informal social networks; on the other hand, the informal social networks provided a basis for the exchange to take place smoothly. In this sense, the multi-actors exchange and the interconnected social structure were two complementary elements in Jinjiang Factory.

From the discussion above, it can be seen that group governance in Jinjiang Factory was a process used to deformalize the formal relations, in which the group leaders' control over their member workers evolved into the leaders' maintenance and management of their social relations. At this point, the consent of production in Jinjiang Factory was distinguished from that argued by Burawoy. In his analysis, the workers' consent of production was rooted in their personal material interest; it was the link between the factory's regime and the workers' income that created the workers' willingness to "make out" (Burawoy 1979). However, in Jinjiang Factory, as well as the personal material interest, social relations also helped in maintaining production. In other words, the workers gave consent to work not merely because of the benefits offered but also, in many cases, because of the social relationships in which they were involved. The material interest emphasizes the economic nature of the man, while the relational interest emphasizes the equal importance of his social nature.

Indeed, workers' exceptional circumstances could not be dealt with without the group leaders' powerful rights in making decisions. At this point, some may question whether, as the lowest-level managers, the group leaders were powerful enough to meet the diverse needs of workers. In other words, even though they were kind enough to show their consideration and understanding to their members, they were not able to give what their member workers needed urgently. Indeed, according to the factory's regulations, even an hour-long absence needed the permission of the workshop, not to mention extending a longer holiday. However, being powerless in front of the formal institutions did not necessarily impede the group leaders from seeking and seizing power by informal means. Although they had no formal rights to authorize leave, they could cheat their leaders by collaborating with their members when it became necessary; they were not allowed to adjust the quota time for each part, but they managed to find ways to balance the skewed interest among members. All these tactics were tacitly understood and accepted by the group leaders and their members. They were absent from any of the factory's *de jure* regulations, and some of them were even harmful to the factory's interests. Even so, it is still unfair and arbitrary simply to equate these informal tactics to misbehavior or conspiracies aimed at resisting their higher managers because these tactics were actually intended to complete their production task better, rather than the opposite.

The example of Jinjiang Factory shows that the group leaders' power derived from these informal rather than formal methods was so influential that, without knowing about it, we can hardly understand how daily production continued smoothly in the face of frequent interruptions. The consideration of exceptional circumstances was a way of governing rather than resisting because it was meant to facilitate rather than disrupt production. It is precisely this informal origin of power that distinguishes this exceptionalism-based system of governance from what has been previously argued. Apparently, to make this system work, two essential resources must be sufficiently owned and effectively controlled by the group leaders: money and time. How, then, did they accumulate these two crucial resources by informal means? This important question is addressed in the next section.

7.4 Tactics for Dealing with the Exceptional Circumstances

David Easton claims that politics is the authoritative allocation of values (Easton 1965). In a way, this reminds us that the ownership of certain allocable "values", material or immaterial, should be the basis of authority. Unauthorized by the formal institutions, the group leaders at Jinjiang Factory sought their allocable values—time and money—informally. Specifically, they were able to earn allocable time from three sources: parceling out jobs, falsifying attendance records, and exploiting "waiting for a job time". The reallocation of members' interests was worked out through the establishment of the group's private coffer, the internal trading of working hours, and the adjustment of the quota time. By using these informal tactics, the group leaders helped their members to deal with the various exceptional circumstances. I now elaborate on these tactics.

Tactics for Time Seeking

Selectively Parceling Out Jobs The primary resource needed to deal with exceptional circumstances was the time that could be given to workers for their non-production needs. Obviously, the direct way to extend non-production time was to shorten working time in the shop. However, the required number of working hours was not determined by the group leaders. As previously mentioned, workers in Jinjiang Factory had to fulfill the required 208 basic working hours, which was calculated by adding the quota time of all processed parts. In this situation, the most effective way to reduce the working time in the shop was to increase the efficiency of unit production. For this purpose, the group leaders parceled out the "easier" jobs to the workers in need of leave. But what jobs were considered "easier"? Basically, keeping the workers' skillfulness and their working conditions constant, the most influential factors were the unit time required to process the part as well as its target volume of production. Usually, the lower the time per unit, the easier the job would be; and the higher the target volume of production, the easier the job. As a result, the easiest job was the one with low processing difficulty and large target production volume.

As already mentioned, except for the Heat Treatment Workshop, workers were assigned tasks based on types of work, such as lathing, grinding, drilling, milling, and planing, rather than types of part. The time required to grind a certain part would vary depending on its type. Take the grinding work in the Machinery Workshop as an example. Figure 7.4 shows the blueprint and quota time card for a screw bolt, which is one part of the oil pump. Figure 7.5 presents the same set of information for the base of the oil pump's delivery valve. According to the record on the quota time card, grinding a screw bolt took 0.16 minutes (procedure code 40), while grinding a delivery-valve base took 0.24 plus 0.30 minutes (procedure

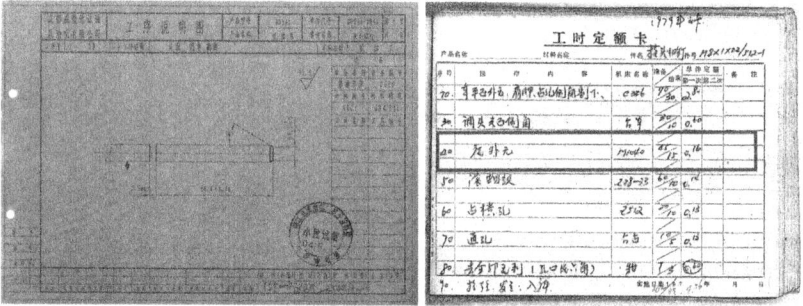

Fig. 7.4 Blueprint and quota time for a screw bolt

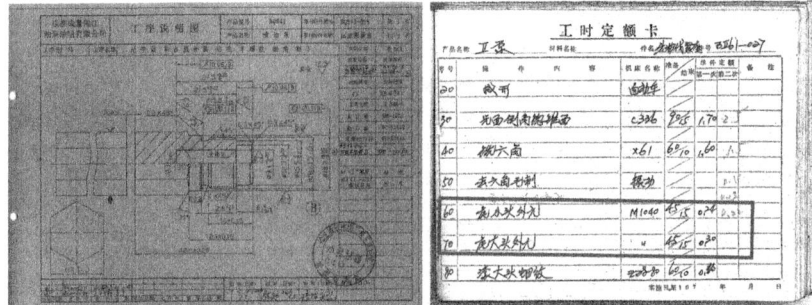

Fig. 7.5 Blueprint and quota time for a delivery-valve base. (Note: On the left is the blueprint, while on the right is the quota time card from 1979. The columns on the quota time card are (left to right): procedure code, content of the procedure, name of the machine tool, time for preparation and finishing, quota time for each unit, and remarks. These two documents were collected by the author in the abandoned Machinery Workshop in June 2013)

code 60 and 70 respectively). It was therefore much easier to grind a screw bolt than a delivery-valve base. Indeed, the accomplishment of a single delivery-valve base accounted for more of the required 208 hours, but working on the much easier screw bolt appeared more likely to increase the efficiency of unit production. Therefore, as the processing volume increased, it would be faster to complete the required working task by doing the easier part.

A larger target volume of production could also help speed up workers' processing progress because, as the quantity increased, proficiency could be enhanced. Another more important reason was the saving in preparation time. Alf Luedtke (1986, p. 68) described the work of turners in a machine construction factory in Chemnitz-Saxony, Germany:

> The turners, however, had to perform a kind of semi-manual labor. Their task was to give each piece its precise shape; therefore, they had to cut notches and to turn threads or screw-joints. To be sure, they did not operate their tools directly by hand, but, similar to the almost artisan-like work of the molders or fitters, they prepared and adjusted the machine, and during the turning of the piece which was to be worked, they intervened, sometimes by hand, especially to file the piece to its final polish. The preparation of the lathe was relatively time-consuming. In order to achieve the optimal speed during the turning process, the gears had to be adjusted and calculated and each time composed anew. The slug then had to be centered;

sometimes it became necessary to put it onto the lathe and trim some splinters by hand-filing. After having started the lathe, the turner had to switch to a mostly passive watchfulness, simultaneously having an eye on the transmission belt and the clutch, the speed of the lathe, and the part of the lathe that carried the cutting or turning tool.

The work in Jinjiang Factory did not differ much from Luedtke's description. From the quota time card in Fig. 7.4, it can be seen that the grinding work for a screw bolt took 0.16 minutes, while its preparation time was up to 45 minutes—281 times longer! In his description, Luedtke points out another advantage that is no less attractive than time conservation: the relatively easy and light work of "passive watchfulness". The part with the larger target production volume was therefore much preferred by workers at Jinjiang Factory.

By parceling out the easier jobs, the group leaders could help their member workers deal with their exceptional circumstances and ensure their completion of the required task at the same time. Thanks to this tactic, not only did the beneficiary acquire extra free time but also had his/her basic interest guaranteed. On this point, group leaders in the Heat Treatment Workshop were in a different situation. Due to its features of teamwork and equal distribution of working hours, the group leaders in this shop had more scope to give extra time to the benefiting worker.

Falsifying the Attendance Record In Jinjiang Factory, the duty of taking attendance records was in the hands of group leaders. The ownership of this power did not make the workers more disciplined; rather it became an effective tool for group leaders to deal with exceptional circumstances. By falsifying the attendance record, they were able to spare the necessary amount of time to the beneficiary workers directly. As one leader said:

> "The phenomenon of getting drunk during the lunch break sometimes happened. Needless to say, it violated the factory's regulations and I should record the absence of those drunken workers in the afternoon. However, in practice, you could be more flexible. To me, I was usually more willing to show them in attendance first, and educate them afterwards. People made mistakes, so as long as they did not make them frequently, I think it could be tolerated."

> "How about the delayed work?" I asked.

> "As for that, I could ask for some help from others in the group, or just do it myself."[6]

This group leader's story provides a vivid illustration of falsifying the attendance record. As a matter of fact, this behavior went on in the groups on a much larger scale than the story seems to suggest. It also can be seen through the leaders' tolerance of their members' sudden absences. As mentioned above, workers at Jinjiang Factory had many reasons to interrupt their work for a short time—to look after their airing quilt, protect their crops, nurse babies, pick up their children, and take a shower in the Heat Treatment Workshop. To tackle this problem, in 1982, the factory enacted a new regulation aimed at reducing the number of workers' sudden absences—anyone who needed to leave work for up to two hours had to apply for an exit pass (Fig. 7.6), noting the exact leaving and returning time. Applications for more than two hours were regarded as time off in lieu, which had to be made up by overtime worked later. The exit pass could only be issued by the workshop leaders. Unfortunately, this apparently strict regulation did not work as well as the factory's leaders expected. As stipulated, workers needed prior permission from their workshop to leave, but they did not need to report upon their return. This serious shortcoming left the group leaders a lot of room for maneuver. As long as the group leaders were able to figure out a way to cover, it was not easy for the workshop leaders, let alone the factory leaders, to know a worker's actual precise time of return. Not surprisingly, it eventually turned out that, although this new regulation was effective in controlling the total number of absences, it did not guarantee the workers' timely return. In fact, leaders even had difficulty reducing the total number of absences. As

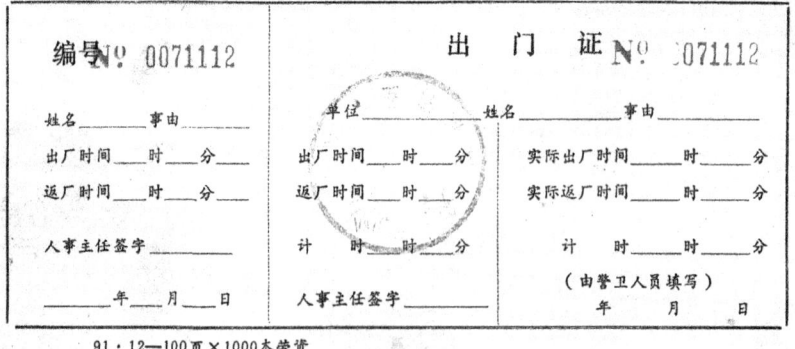

Fig. 7.6 Scanned exit pass

mentioned in previous chapters, workers at Jinjiang Factory were inter-connected by internal clanization. Despite the existence of certain bound-aries between workers, the exchanges enabled by these networks of social relationships appeared extensive enough for some workers to secure an exit pass and get around the gatekeepers' watch. To solve these problems, the factory leaders did take some measures, but many did not work. The following are Tan Yi's conference notes on the exit pass between 1982 and 1987:

July 5, 1982 Meeting of Workshop Party Secretaries
The exit pass could only be issued by the Director or Party Secretary of each workshop.

August 7, 1982 Meeting of Workshop Personnel Directors
If anyone needed the exit pass for time off in lieu, it could not be granted without the signature of the workshop leaders. Every workshop leader must apply this rule very firmly.

October 6, 1983 Meeting of Workshop Personnel Directors
The application for the exit pass needed an acceptable reason, such as time off in lieu or sick leave. In the application, the applicant must clearly state the return time. Upon return, the applicants needed to sign in at the factory's gatekeepers.

March 2, 1984 Meeting of Group Leaders in the Heat Treatment Workshop
1) Group leaders took the shift to supervise the workshop production and discipline. 2) Anyone who needed the exit pass for time off in lieu should get his group leaders' agreement first, and then submit the applica-tion to the workshop.

June 28, 1987 Meeting of the Group Leaders in the Heat Treatment Workshop
Any leave [taken] without [an] application would result in the deduction of group points, one point each time. If the group leaders could make up the application the next morning, the deduction could be exempted once. In addition, every group needed to submit the shift schedule to the work-shop. By the end of each month, the salary officer collected all sorts of docu-ments on the leave issue, including the exit passes. The workshop discipline team was composed of Tan, Chen and He.

November 29, 1987. Some Supplementary Regulations on the Working Discipline
The exit pass, business leave and one-day sick leave could only be approved by the workshop leaders. Sick leave of more than one day was regarded as time off in lieu. Every workshop leader must be careful with and accountable for their authorizations.

In Tan's conference notes, three points emerge from the factory's regulations regarding the exit pass. First, the power of issuing the exit pass should be in the hands of workshop leaders; second, the ethics of leaders could not be overlooked; third, the group leaders were required to cooperate with the workshop leaders. Only the third point specified the role of group leaders. In doing so, the workshop made an attempt to equate the group interest with that of every individual member. However, there is no reason to believe that such an attempt was effective in reducing rather than increasing the cheating behavior of group leaders. In any event, the repeated emphasis placed on the issue of the exit pass at least revealed two things: on the one hand, the problem of workers' sudden absences was not effectively solved by the regulation of exit passes; on the other hand, the factory leaders had not remedied the weaknesses of the regulation. Interestingly, although its ineffectiveness was common knowledge in the factory, the exit pass policy was canceled following its introduction. All interviewees made similar comments that "Indeed, it had some problems, but you cannot deny that it also had some positive effects."

Exploiting "Waiting for a Job Time" If the above two tactics were direct ways of sparing time for the beneficiary workers, the exploitation of "waiting for a job time" was an indirect way to allocate free time among members. Basically, the time spent waiting for jobs is the unoccupied period created by the discontinuity of job provision. According to the factory regulations, workers unoccupied for this period should be reported to the workshop by their group leaders. During this period, in order to fully use the labor, the workshop would assign them to do some non-production work, such as cleaning the workshop floor, sorting out documents, and so on. All these tasks were called "jobs without quota time" (*wu ding'e gong-zuo*). In other words, no matter how much work of this kind was done, it would not be counted toward the required 208 hours. Obviously, workers waiting for job were very reluctant to offer their labor for these duties. The group leaders also had no incentive to abide strictly by the factory's regulation to transfer their own labor to the workshop, even though this was temporary. Instead, they were more willing to give the workers half a day off, or even more, without informing their senior managers. In so doing, the group leaders effectively increased the possibility of securing the cooperation of these benefiting workers in the foreseeable future. Once exceptional circumstances came up for some other members, they were more likely to be mobilized to contribute more labor in the group to make up for the potential loss. In a word, by exploiting the "waiting for a job time", the group leaders successfully expanded their governable time. This extra free time worked like a loan paid by the leaders and continually transferred and consumed among their members. In this way, the members' many exceptional circumstances could be accepted without affecting the whole group's production. It should be reemphasized that this continued exchange behavior should not be understood in a purely rational way. On the face of it, the regular give-and-take interactions appealed to the workers' rationality. However, in fact, the value of each give and take was not the same. Many instances of the workers' help could not even be calculated. It was the value inequality that reflected the irrational elements of this exchange. In other words, it was not out of workers' purely rational calculations. In addition, this exchange system should not be regarded as an intentional design by the group leaders. It was more like a strategy evolved through the day-to-day interactions and shaped by the particular situations rather than a product of intentional design.

In a word, parceling out jobs selectively, falsifying attendance records and the exploitation of time spent waiting for jobs were three implicit but not unimportant tactics by which the group leaders were able to spare their member workers some extra free time, either directly or indirectly, to deal with the multifarious "exceptional circumstances". However, time could not solve everything. In the factory, time usually meant money: tolerance of one person's absence might harm the whole group's interests; giving easier tasks to a certain worker might also lead to an imbalance in interests among the member workers. Therefore, as they sought more free time, the group leaders also needed to find effective ways to prevent their members' interests from being jeopardized too much.

Tactics for Balancing the Workers' Interest

Building up the Private Coffer Needless to say, money was the most effective tool for balancing the interests of workers. But where could the group leaders obtain this extra money for their own disposal? In Jinjiang

Factory, almost all the production groups had built up a private coffer (*xiaojinku*). Money in the private coffer could be accumulated in two main ways. The first and foremost was by holding back some portion of the group bonus. The group bonus came from exceeding production and should somehow be distributed among its members. However, the group leaders only distributed part of the bonus and kept the rest for the group's "unexpected needs" (*bushizhixu*). This sum of money was usually kept by the leaders in a semi-transparent way, which means that, even though the members knew their leaders would keep some money in reserve, they did not know how much was taken away. This ambiguity was maintained by the "double-blind" policy of bonus distribution under which the bonus was usually sealed in an envelope. The specific amount was strictly confidential and workers were not supposed to ask what it was. This meant that the workers could not find out the amount from either official channels or their own calculations. The second source of money was through falsifying overtime. At the end of every month, the group leaders were asked to report their group's total hours of overtime, for which the workshop gave overtime pay to each group. In this process, the group leaders usually tended to report as many hours as they could. The difference in payment between reported and actual overtime was retained by the leaders. For this purpose, they falsified the overtime records as a matter of routine. It was not unusual, for example, to record an hour of actual overtime as one and half hours.

The workshop leaders were not unaware of these cheating behaviors, but they did not take them seriously. In their eyes, they were understandable and acceptable. Moreover, some of them even implicitly encouraged the creation of private coffers. As the Director of the Machining Workshop commented:

> Actually, we all knew they (group leaders) were building up their own private coffers. And we also knew where they obtained the money. But we did not take measures to forbid them. In the workshop, the group leaders were the ones who had immediate contact with workers. Their work was very heavy and complicated because they had to get along well with every member in the group. Even one troublemaker could be a headache for the whole group. As a result, besides their production work, the most important task for these leaders was to unite their members by whatever means. In order to do this, eating and drinking were unavoidable. You could not expect these

leaders to pay out of their own pockets. Actually, in my workshop, we even had a budget for this private coffer money. It was usually given to the group leaders together with their group bonus.[7]

As this interviewee's comments showed, support from the workshop management might be the main reason for the development of the group's private coffer. With the coffer, the group leaders grasped more available resources, which provided them with more choices in dealing with the relations with their member workers. Perhaps, in this director's eyes, food and drink were the main methods employed by the group leaders. In fact, however, they were just two of many. As their autonomy increased, the group leaders developed more tactics to balance their members' interests, some of which even contradicted their senior managers' interests.

Trading in Working Hours Trading working hours was an exchange carried out among different members in one group. It usually occurred when someone in the group could not complete the required 208 hours for whatever reason. The process could be summarized as having four steps: first, the group leader obtained a worker's agreement to be the donor; second, the donor worker wrote his/her excess working hours on the recipient's work-ticket (*gongpiao*); third, when the bonus was awarded, the recipient worker took the basic bonus for the completion of the 208 hours, while the donor worker took the rest; fourth, the group leader gave the donor worker a subsidy from the private coffer. In this way, the group members were able to minimize the loss of workers and the group. More importantly, in cases where the trade was due to the recipient's long-term absence, it was also a way to disguise the actual length of the absence. In this sense, the trading of working hours within the group could also be a tactic for sparing more free time. A by-product of this mutual help was the strengthening of internal cohesion, not only between the leaders and their members but also among the members.

Adjusting the Quota Time Although the quota time was determined with reference to previous production records, it was impossible to be completely accurate. The condition of machinery, quality of materials, skillfulness of workers, and so on were all possible factors that influenced the actual working time. If the quota time was longer than the actually required working time, it was called a "loose quota" (*ding'e song*); other-wise, it was regarded as a "tight quota" (*ding'ejin*). In day-to-day work, nobody had better knowledge of this than the workers themselves. Needless to say, everyone was more willing to work on the part with a loose quota and no one wanted to be at a disadvantage. Having no right to change the quota time, group leaders usually had two ways to deal with the potential imbalance in interests. On the one hand, they could move the easier work in turn among members; on the other hand, they could adjust the hourly rate of the excess bonus for different tasks. In Jinjiang Factory, the latter was more popular among group leaders. As one leader recalled, "If the quota time of one task was recognized as loose, we would lower its bonus of each excess hour, for example from 1.2 yuan to 1 yuan; otherwise, we would raise it."[8]This was taken by the group leaders as their unofficial adjustment of the quota time. In this way, the group leaders avoided potential disputes over imbalanced interests. More importantly, by matching the quota time with the adjusted excess bonus, group leaders were able to freely parcel out jobs according to some particular need without compromising others' interests. This released more autonomous space for the group leaders.

In essence, in dealing with the various exceptional circumstances, the group leaders sought to expand their autonomy outside what the formal institution allowed. With this autonomy, they were able to figure out some tactics to provide their members with extra free time and protect their interests from being harmed. However, the employment of these tactics would inevitably damage the factory's interests. Faced with this problem, the factory and workshop leaders appeared to be in an irreconcilable dilemma: on the one hand, they were conscious of the negative effects of these tactics; on the other hand, they also admitted the necessity of some of these tactics. As a result, they always took an equivocal attitude toward such behavior. In this sense, the acquiescence of the higher management also fostered the growth of a series of tactics within the group. But it was these tactics that strengthened connections within the group by which the basic production could be maintained without being seriously affected by the continuous interruptions.

7.5   Conclusion

In this chapter, I illustrated the tolerating strategy through the example of absenteeism management in Jinjiang Factory. It embodied the group leaders' tolerance and consideration toward every member's exceptional circumstances. In so doing, the leaders won the members' recognition and support. More importantly, through the solicitation of others' assistance, this tolerance and consideration was exchanged among members, through which the group's internal cohesion was gradually strengthened. Of course, this form of governance could not function without substantial material support. In order to accumulate as many resources as possible, group leaders invented a series of tactics. These helped them to provide their members with more free time while maintaining their income at a certain level. In a word, it was the toleration that strengthened the group's internal connections and guaranteed the basic production in the face of interruptions.

The benign feature of governance at Jinjiang Factory was even more evident when compared to the neo-traditionalism and disorganized despotism in urban factories. Walder (1986, p. 108) indicated that, in many urban SOEs, "Employees whose slack performance threatens the attainment of group goals will first be talked to informally by the group leader, and if no change results, the employee will be criticized and called on to justify his or her lax performance in a group meeting." In addition, there is also a definite material incentive for other group members to report and criticize lax behavior (Walder 1986).

Zhao and Nichols found that the managerial control of labor attendance at the cotton mills of Henan province in the 1980s was even harsher. According to their observations, these mills introduced two mechanisms to tighten the management's control: control over sick leave and the exercise of monetary sanctions against those who took leave, whether due to sickness or on compassionate grounds (Zhao and Nichols 1996, p. 10).

In terms of the comparisons above, it can be seen that toleration as a governing strategy in Third Line Enterprises departs from the conventional wisdom of managerial control in at least three crucial aspects. First, most previous studies implicitly assume the vertical integration and homogeneity of management, while the toleration model assumes otherwise. In the analyses of neo-traditionalism and disorganized despotism, the interest of group leaders is either overlooked or taken to overlap with that of their senior managers. On the contrary, this study shows that the group leaders' interest is not predetermined, but created and shaped in the course of their constant interaction with their senior managers and member workers. On the lowest rung of management, the group leaders have to complete the stipulated production task; as the head of a group, they have to seek ways to secure their members' consent to work. From the perspective of their member workers, on the one hand, they are managers who are supposed to strictly enforce the factory's regulations on absenteeism, but, on the other hand, they are also friends or even relatives who are expected to forgive breaches of the rules. With these multiple roles and expectations, group leaders resort to a strategy that is neither obedient nor defiant in nature: they complete the required production task through some vicious tactics that are detrimental to the factory's interest. In so doing, they place their group interest above the factory interest.

Second, in previous analyses, workers' rule-breaking behavior is taken as an impediment to the management, while this study, as the example of absenteeism management showed above, considers it as a commodity exchanged between group leaders and workers for the purpose of labor control. Rather than passively accepting the formal institutions, workers and group leaders actively invent a series of hidden rules, tacit knowledge, and informal tactics to minimize the potential tensions. In the case of absence management, one significant hidden rule was the multi-actors exchange mechanism employed in dealing with the contradiction between the production and workers' absences. The tacit knowledge was the shared understanding of workers' exceptional circumstances. The informal tactics referred to all the tactics taken by group leaders to seek more allocable time and money. It is these invisible and informal agreements that dominate the quotidian life of workers and their immediate managers.

Third, in contrast to the previously argued governance that usually occurs between two parties, the toleration model presents a novel one taken place among multiple actors. In Walder's neo-traditionalism, the group governance is mainly dependent on the patron–client link between group leaders and activists. In Lee's disorganized despotism, managers employ coercive means over all their workers. The toleration model, however, operates between the coordinator, the favor donor, and the favor taker. This governing strategy can be hardly realized between two parties because neither the coordinator nor the donor can independently provide the favor to the taker. The group leaders, who in practice are the coordinators, need the assistance of other member workers to satisfy the need of the taker, while the donor workers have to gain their group leaders' permission, officially or implicitly, to provide their help. In so doing, the favor, usually in the form of free time and monetary income, is rotated among these three actors.

Some may suspect that the gradual but drastic reforms of the 1980s might alter the governing strategy formed prior to the reform era.

However, this change did not occur in Jinjiang Factory. By contrast, some of the reforms might even strengthen the existing form of governance. First, similar to what many scholars have presented, managers at Jinjiang Factory were not able freely to fire their workers. In other words, Jinjiang Factory workers during the reform era still enjoyed job security. Ma Jie's case, presented in the previous chapter, provides typical evidence on this point. Second, the development of the foreign-invested and domestic private sectors in southeast China provided workers with more opportunities in larger cities, which placed great pressure on the management to maintain its workforce. According to a deputy director at Jinjiang Factory, by 1984, 582 workers had left the factory, of which 81 were technicians.[9] In a conference on human resources in April 1984, the factory received as many as 146 applications to leave. As a result, in order to prevent more and more workers from leaving, managers had to respond quickly to workers' demands. In essence, the 1980s reforms, which aimed to promote productivity in the factory, actually increased workers' bargaining power. The toleration, as a governing strategy, was therefore able to remain.

NOTES

1. At this point, the reinterpretation of absenteeism as the exceptional circumstances shares the philosophical basis of the *Renqing*, which was argued by Zhai Xuewei (2013).
2. Interview with Fu Jinhai.
3. Interview with Fu Jinhai, Chen Mingzhen, Fang Mingqi, and GuJiwei.
4. Interview with Fu Jinhai, Chen Mingzhen, Fang Mingqi, and GuJiwei.
5. Interview with Zhu Baogui.
6. Interview with Fang Wensheng.
7. Interview with Gu Jiwei.
8. Interview with Fang Wensheng.
9. Interview with Yu Xuehui.

REFERENCES

Bourdieu, Pierre. 1977. *Outline of a Theory of Practice*, Cambridge: Cambridge University Press.

Burawoy, Michael. 1979. *Manufacturing Consent: Changes in the Labor Process Under Monopoly Capitalism*, Chicago: University of Chicago Press.

Bian, Yanjie. 1997. Bring Strong Ties Back in: Indirect Ties, Network Bridges, and Job Searches in China, *American Sociological Review*, 62(3):366–85.

Chan, Anita and Jonathan Unger. 1982 (Fall). Grey and Black: The Hidden Economy of Rural China, *Pacific Affairs*, 55(3):452–71.

Easton, David. 1965. *Systems of Analysis of Political Life*, New York: John Wiley and Sons.

Ekeh, Peter P. 1974. *Social Exchange Theory: The Two Traditions*, London: Heinemann Educational Books Ltd.

Luedtke, Alf. 1986. Cash, Coffee-Breaks, Horseplay: 'Eigensinn' and Politics Among Factory Workers in Germany circa 1900, in Hanagan, Michael and Charles Stephenson, eds. *Confrontation, Class Consciousness, and the Labor Process*, Westport: Greenwood Press, 65–96.

Solinger, Dorothy. 1983. Marxism and Market in Socialist China: The Reforms of 1979–1980 in Context, in Nee, Victor and David Mozingo, eds. *State and Society in Contemporary China*, Ithaca: Cornell University Press, 194–219

Walder, Andrew G. 1986. *Communist Neo-Traditionalism: Work and Authority in Chinese Industry*, Berkeley: University of California Press.

Womack, Brantly. 1991 (June). Transfigured Community: Neo-Traditionalism and Work Unit Socialism in China, *The China Quarterly*, 126:313–332.

Wasserman, Stanley and Katherine Faust. 1994. *Social Network Analysis: Methods and Approaches*, Cambridge: Cambridge University Press.

Yang, Mayfair Mei-hui. 1989 (January). The Gift Economy and State Power in China, *Comparative Studies in Society and History*, 31(1):25–54.

Zhao, Minghua and Theo Nichols. 1996 (July). Management Control of Labor in State-Owned Enterprises: Cases from the Textile Industry, *The China Journal*, 36:1–21.

Zhou, Xueguang. 1999. Review on the Studies of Institutional Change of Chinese Organizations in Western Sociology, *The Study of Sociology*, 4:26–43.

Zhai, Xuewei. 2013. *Face, Favor and Reproduction of Power*, Beijing: Beijing University Press.

CHAPTER 8

Conclusion

In every respect, the Third Line Construction has undoubtedly been of great importance to the development of Chinese industry. It was so huge a project that it involved three quarters of China's provinces and millions of its citizens. In spite of its initial military and security motivations, the national movement had a general impact on the local economy, culture, education, and technology of central and western China. However, this significant event has not yet received much attention from academia. Despite the numerous works on Chinese labor, the Third Line workers remain largely absent from the existing literature. Motivated by the empirical significance and theoretical overview, this book represents a first attempt to explore the politics and sociology of the Third Line workers by answering the following core question: What were industrial relations like in the Third Line Enterprises? How were they formed? In this study I have shown that, although the geographic isolation of Third Line Enterprises cut off pre-existing social relationships among workers, it did not give managers greater leverage over their workers. Instead, managers had to adapt by tolerating workers' rule-breaking actions. This toleration was rooted in three contextual conditions.

First and foremost was their isolation from the outside world. Located in remote mountainous areas, the Third Line Enterprises operated as independent and fully functional societies. This isolated living condition directly led to the interconnected social networks and forced workers in Third Line Enterprises to seek their friends and marital partners within the factory. However, this process did not occur at random. Usually, the

C. Chen, *Toleration*, New Perspectives on Chinese Politics and Society, https://doi.org/10.1007/978-981-10-8941-1_8

workforce of Third Line Enterprises was mainly composed of three subgroups: transferred workers, Returned Educated Youths, and demobilized soldiers. Moreover, this division was further deepened by their job niches in the factory. In their constant and immediate day-to-day interactions, workers of each group frequently created certain group characteristics and drew boundaries between "us" and "them" (Crang 1998, p. 60), consciously or subconsciously. As a result, even though each group of workers was not a completely closed circle, workers were more likely to build their social relations within the group they belonged to. Over time, the deep and strong ties within the group strengthened its internal solidarity. Ties across groups, despite being less common, nevertheless existed and made the workers of different groups interconnected in one way or another. In the face of the rich informal relations, the grass-roots managers were very reluctant to enforce formal regulations strictly on their member workers, which gave rise to the rampant absenteeism and forced the leaders to come up with a more flexible form of management.

If the interconnected social networks had somehow unintentionally empowered the ordinary workers, the various means of control over production were deliberately sought by workers to increase their power. Thanks to their permanent employment status and immobility across positions, workers were able to learn how to control the pace of work and maintain their income at the same time. For example, they could reorder the sequence of processing, recalibrate the quota task among different parts, and make use of any uncoordinated actions or plans in the factory. All these autonomies were self-discovered through routine day-to-day working experience in the shop, serving as a set of informal and tacit knowledge beneath the seemingly well-controlled formal institutions. In these circumstances, the group leader's authority was never full-fledged but was in fact constrained by the workers' self-empowerment. Therefore, instead of rigidly exerting their power on member workers, group leaders were more willing to resort to a flexible method. The relationship between key concepts in this work is presented in Fig. 8.1.

In order better to illustrate how the toleration manifested itself in day-to-day management, I take the governance of absenteeism at Jinjiang Factory as an example. As discussed in the previous chapter, the strategy of tolerance toward the management of absenteeism was based on three building blocks. First, it was a reinterpretation and justification of a worker's absence as being due to his/her exceptional circumstance. Being drunk during working hours, going home for farm work or looking after children, taking care of airing a quilt or protecting crops from bad weather,

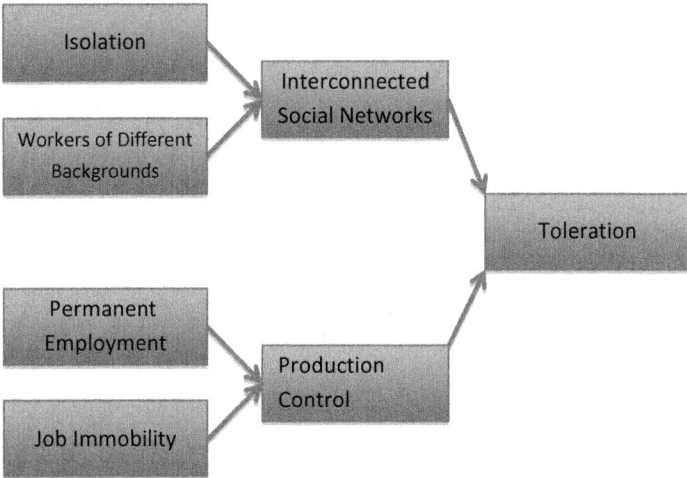

Fig. 8.1   Relationship between key concepts

and so on were all typical examples of exceptional circumstances used to justify absenteeism. Since it was difficult to rank these exceptional circumstances in terms of urgency and importance, they were equally tolerated as valid excuses for absence.

Second, in order to cover the absentees' tasks, group leaders initiated an exchange between multiple actors. One crucial feature of this exchange was the group leaders acting simultaneously as the favor donor and taker. They donated their consideration and tolerance to the absent worker, while having to seek the help of other member workers to complete the production tasks. The second feature of this exchange was that it was not reciprocal in the classical sense of the word. That is, the favor would not necessarily be returned to the same person who donated the help. Instead, the exchange took place in the form of "favor-pooling" among member workers. In this process, those who offered help did so out of their gratitude for the assistance they had previously received from their group leaders and other member colleagues through the favor pool, and those who received help would engage in favor-pooling by providing help to others in the future. This non-reciprocal flow of social capital allowed the exchange among multiple actors to continue and therefore made the toleration strategy work. In this respect, toleration and its operating mechanism—the tripartite exchange—were not fully based on rationality but had many emotional elements.

Of course, this multiple-actor exchange could not work without some necessary resources. The tactics to sustain the exchange were the third building block of the tolerance strategy. In previous chapters, I introduced two types of resources that group leaders sought to accumulate. The first is time. Generally speaking, group leaders expanded the time at their disposal by exploiting production processes in three ways: selectively parceling out jobs among member workers, falsifying attendance records, and taking advantage of "waiting for a job time". The second resource crucial to the group governance is money, which was also accumulated in three ways in the course of production. Group leaders built up their private coffers, coordinated the trading of working hours among different member workers, and privately adjusted quota times. None of these tactics were permitted by the factory's formal regulations, but they were the living dynamics beneath the quiet surface in the workshop. These tactics were desirable because they could be used by group leaders to mobilize their members in completing the work; they were undesirable, however, because they damaged the interests of the factory as a whole. It was this paradoxical effect that defined the formation of grass-roots managers' governance: the interest of the group was always above the interest of the factory. In this sense, the group leader was never an accountable client of their senior bosses. Therefore, any analysis of industrial relations in China from the patron–client perspective[1] is questionable without clarifying how such managerial dilemma has been solved or how its existence affects day-to-day operations.

8.1   Varieties of Industrial Authority

What is the novelty of toleration as a model for a system of industrial governance? Basically, it differs from two others—neo-traditionalism and disorganized despotism—in two respects. First, in the practice of the tolerance strategy, the numerous and constant absences were seen by group leaders as a resource to unite members and strengthen the group's internal interest, while in the other two governance regimes, absenteeism was simply seen as an obstacle to management and production. As argued in previous chapters, through the reinterpretation and equal tolerance of absences due to personal exceptional circumstances, group leaders were able to win their members' trust and support; through the exchange of favors, group members' interests were deeply connected in the favor pool. In this respect, rampant absenteeism was not necessarily an impediment to the group management. Instead, it was exploited as an instrument to complete the group's production tasks. In previous studies on China's industrial governance, however, absenteeism is always negatively portrayed. In neo-traditionalism, it is understood as immoral and treacherous behavior (Walder 1986); in the despotic workplaces, it is also strictly forbidden due to its adverse impacts on production (Lee 1998).

Second, a strategy of tolerance emphasized the independent interest of the production group and the group leader, while the other two governing regimes simply viewed the group leaders as the lowest policy implementers and ignored their autonomy. I have shown in previous chapters that the governing principle of toleration and its underpinning tactics were beneficial to the group but harmful to the factory. They were not enacted by the factory's top-level policymakers but invented by the group leaders in response to the social, political, and production environments. Therefore, the interest of groups and group leaders was not predetermined but figured out by the leaders and their member workers through day-to-day interactions. In this sense, the interests of the grass-roots management and its upper management did not overlap as previous studies have assumed. Thus the bipolar opposition between managers and workers according to the Marxist functionalist approach is also problematic.

In view of the discussion above, it can be seen that tolerance as a novel industrial authority was not only a response to macro-political, social, and economic structures but also an adaptive product of the micro day-to-day interactions among agents. These complicated dynamics jointly affected the power parity between the two main groups of actors discussed in this work, group leaders and their workers. My empirical evidence indicates that, in Third Line Enterprises, leaders were not so strong and workers not so weak. It is this relatively equal power distribution that made mutual adjustment a viable option, which eventually gave rise to a strategy that prioritized the interests of the group as a whole. If we categorize industrial regimes in terms of the power parity or disparity between group leaders and member workers, we may be able to hypothesize three categories of the regime for the future test, as summarized in Table 8.1.

Table 8.1   Categories of industrial regimes

		Strength of member workers	
		Strong	*Weak*
Strength of group leaders	*Strong*	Accommodating mode	Suppressive mode
	Weak	Responsive mode	N.A.

The balance of power between group leaders and their member workers was more likely to produce the accommodating mode of management, such as the tolerance in the Third Line Enterprises argued in this study. In factories of this kind, the group interest as a whole was exogenous to the factory interest and the former was usually placed above the latter. Under the suppressive mode, group leaders were more powerful than their workers, and they tended to employ suppressive means in dealing with workers' misbehavior, such as the case of neo-traditionalism in urban SOEs (Walder 1986) and the despotic regimes in foreign-invested firms and other small private workplaces (Lee 1998; Pun 2005; Pun and Smith 2007; Chan 2010; Wallis 2013). These regimes were the most likely in which the group interest converged with the factory interest. Finally, if workers were more powerful than their leaders, group leaders faced big challenges from their members and tended to be more responsive to their members' demands. Under the responsive mode, ordinary workers' interests were taken seriously, which could even result in adjustment of the factory's policies related to the introduction of new production and techniques. Chen (2006, 2008) has done some preliminary work on this type of management regime in village Enterprises.

The varieties of industry authorities imply that industrial relations are highly contingent on their contexts. Even in factories of the same ownership, such as urban SOEs and the Third Line Enterprises, the internal political dynamics could be so different that any argument established in one context needs to be reconsidered and revised in another.

8.2   Does Dependency Lead to Obedience?

It has been widely accepted that, prior to the market-oriented reforms, the obedient nature of the permanently employed workers in Chinese SOEs was due to their organized dependence. On this point, Andrew Walder makes the most forceful assertion. According to him, the organized dependence was an institutional feature of Chinese SOEs, which included three sub-aspects. First, workers were assumed to be immobile and economically dependent on their Enterprises; second, they were politically monopolized by the party and the management of the factory; and, third, they were personally supervised by their immediate leaders, with many conceivable needs and benefits (Walder 1986, p. 13). As a result, the *danwei* (work unit)—the collective name of all the workplaces—turns out to be a locus of the state-controlling techniques that combined disciplinary and normative forms of control (Yang 1989; Lu 1989; Li 1993; Li 2004).

On the surface, workers at the Third Line Enterprises do not seem different from their urban counterparts. Living in a remote area isolated from the outside world, they could even be more dependent on their workplace. However, as previous chapters have shown, in stark contrast to what previous studies have argued, the greater dependence of the workers in Third Line Enterprises did not make them easier to manage. Absenteeism was a serious problem for the factory's management. I have argued that this puzzling phenomenon can be explained by two featured social dynamics. First, the connivance of absenteeism was due to the labeled clanization; second, it was tacitly allowed because of the group leaders' full awareness of the members' hidden autonomies in the production process.

These two pieces of novel ethnographical evidence heuristically enrich our knowledge of Chinese labor politics in two ways. First, the labor division in the Third Line Enterprises shows that, unlike the claims of previous studies, the heterogeneity of workers cannot be neatly determined by their skill profiles, level of education, or places of origin,[2] or by their occupational or socioeconomic status.[3] Instead, the division is also embedded in the sub-identities, such as transferred workers, Returned Educated Youth, and demobilized soldiers. Even though these multifarious sub-identities were created unintentionally through several state-mobilized movements, they are intentionally differentiated by the government's socioeconomic policies. As shown in earlier chapters, in Jinjiang Factory, these three groups of workers were subject to very different training systems and wage policies. This fragmentation was perceived and further solidified in the immediate day-to-day interactions. These sub-identities were so hard transcended that they had powerful political and sociological impact on relations between management and labor.

Second, this study shows that the ordinary workers were not passive recipients, but active agents capable of exploiting the formal policies for personal gain. On the topic of Chinese labor, previous studies are constrained by a dichotomous analytical framework. In these analyses, Chinese workers are either obedient or resistant. However, the experience of workers in Jinjiang Factory shows us that they were neither fully willing to comply with orders nor radical enough to stir up collective protests. Instead, they were located in between, seeking strategies and tactics to expand their personal benefits. As described in the previous chapters, workers in Jinjiang workshops explore their hidden autonomies in production. These behaviors are not obedient in nature because they are usually damaging to the factory's interests nor should they be regarded as resistant because they do not intentionally challenge authority. The key issue in the workshop, therefore, is not how to produce docile workers or how to deal with sporadic, more-symbolic-than-meaningful collective resistance but how to seek out and respond appropriately to those covert, flexible, and resilient misbehaviors. In this respect, a certain industrial authority is endogenous to the dynamics of daily production practices.

Does dependence lead to obedience? This study indicates that this question cannot be answered in a general way. Without in-depth knowledge of how the different types of social networks were interwoven in the factory and how the power relations were reconstructed by active agents in the workshop, generalization may risk leading us further from the truth.

NOTES

1. On the patron–client ties in SOEs, see Walder, Andrew G. 1986. *Communist Neo-Traditionalism*; for a village perspective, see the representative work by Jean Oi, 1989, *State and Peasant in Contemporary China*.
2. Perry's (1993) work is a representative one on the role of places of origin.
3. See, for example, Perry 1994. In this article, Perry mentioned the difference between the permanent employment workers and the temporary workers.

REFERENCES

Crang, Mike. 1998. *Cultural Geography*, London: Routledge.

Chan, Chris King-Chi. 2010. *The Challenge of Labor in China: Strikes and the Changing Labor Regime in Global Factories*, London and New York: Routledge.

Chen, Calvin. 2006. Work, Conformity, and Defiance: Strategies of Resistance and Control in China's Township and Village Enterprises, in Eyferth, Jacob, ed. *How China Works: Perspectives on the Twentieth-century Industrial Workplace*, London and New York: Routledge.

Chen, Calvin. 2008. *Some Assembly Required: Work, Community and Politics in China's Rural Enterprises*, Cambridge: Harvard University Asia Center.

Lu, Feng, 1989. Danwei: A Unique Form of Social Organization, *Chinese Social Science*, 1:71–88.

Li, Hanlin. 1993. China's Danwei Phenomenon and the Mechanisms of Conformity in Urban Communities, *Sociology Research*, 5:23–32.

Li, Hanlin. 2004. *Chinese Danwei Society: Discussion, Thinking and Research,* Shanghai: Shanghai People's Press.

Lee, Ching-Kwan. 1998. *Gender and the South China Miracle: Two Worlds of Factory Women,* London: University of California Press.

Oi, C. Jean. 1989. *State and Peasant in Contemporary China: The Political Economy of Village Government,* Berkeley and Los Angeles: University of California Press.

Perry, Elizabeth. 1993. *Shanghai on Strike: The Politics of Chinese Labor,* Stanford: Stanford University Press.

Perry, Elizabeth. 1994 (March). Shanghai's Strike Wave of 1957, *The China Quarterly,* 137:1–27.

Pun, Ngai. 2005. *Made in China: Women Factory Workers in a Global Workplace,* Durham: Duke University Press.

Pun, Ngai and Chris Smith. 2007. Putting Transnational Labor Process in Its Place: The Dormitory Labor Regime in Post-Socialist China, *Work, Employment Society,* 21 (1):27–45.

Walder, Andrew G. 1986. *Communist Neo-Traditionalism: Work and Authority in Chinese Industry,* Berkeley: University of California Press.

Wallis, Cara. 2013. *Technomobility in China: Young Migrant Women and Mobile Phones,* New York and London: New York University Press.

Yang, Mayfair Mei-hui. 1989. Between the State and Society: The Construction of Corporateness in a Chinese Socialist Factory, *Australian Journal of Chinese Affairs,* 22:31–60.

APPENDIX: THE SOCIAL RELATIONS OF L'S AND C'S FAMILIES IN THE FACTORY

L's Family (Returned Educated Youth)

L's family had three brothers, LZS, LZH, and LY. LZS worked in the Department of Quality Control and his wife ZKX worked in the factory's hospital. LZH worked in the Department of Human Resource and his wife WLF worked in the Department of Design. LY was once the director of the Workshop of Casting and Forging.

LZS had one daughter and one son. His daughter, LYH, worked as a grinder in the Workshop of Machining and her husband WWD was once the director of Workshop of Preparation. LZS's son, LYY, worked in the Department of Finance and his wife LCY worked in the Department of Design. LZS also had a brother-in-law, LRS, who worked in the Workshop of Machining. Like LZS, LRS also had one daughter and one son. His daughter, LSJ, worked in the Workshop of Machining. LRS's son, LSW, worked in the Workshop of Machining as well.

LZH has a cousin, ZY, who was an electrician in the Workshop of Machining. LY's brother-in-law, ZT, was once the director of Department of Human Resource. Z's wife, XF was the factory's statistician. XF's nephew, XY, worked in the factory's Union and his wife XGR was a worker in the Workshop of Machining. The social relations of L's family is shown in Fig. A1.

© The Author(s) 2018
C. Chen, *Toleration*, New Perspectives on Chinese Politics and Society, https://doi.org/10.1007/978-981-10-8941-1

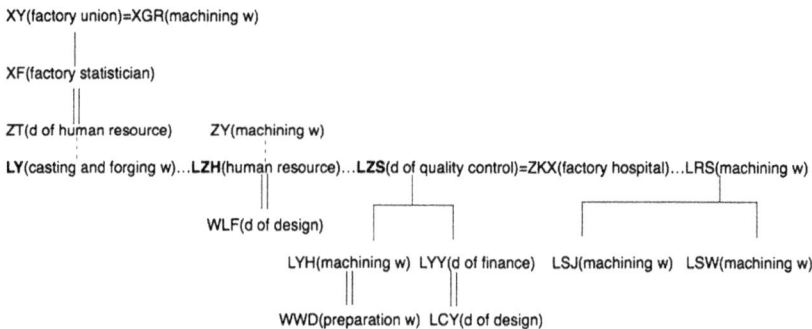

Fig. A1   L's social relations in the factory. (Notes: In this figure, "=" denotes marriage relationship; "…" denotes the relationship of siblings; "_" linking different names indicates people across generations, but not necessarily the parent–child relations. "W" denotes "workshop", while "d" denotes "department")

C's Family (Transferred Workers)

CZY was once the vice director of Jinjiang Factory. His wife, JGE, worked in the factory's warehouse. They had three daughters, CJH, CJL, and CJG. They also had two sons, CJP and CJN.

CJH worked in the Assembly Shop and her husband, ZJZ, was a worker in the Workshop of Instrument. ZJZ's father ZGS worked in the factory's Instrument Office. ZJZ's mother, ZXF, was the factory's accountant. ZJZ had a sister, ZLM, who worked in the workshop of Matching. Her husband, SYS, worked in the Assembly Shop. S's father, SZ, was once the vice director of Department of Logistics.

CJL and her husband worked in the Workshop of Heat Treatment. CJG worked in the Workshop of Matching, while her husband HJJ worked in the Workshop of Instrument.

CJP was a fitter in the Workshop of Instrument and his wife, CJQ, worked in the Department of Sales. CJN was a driver in the Department of Transportation and his wife, ZH, worked in the Workshop of Instrument. ZH's father, ZQS, worked in the Department of Transportation as well and ZH's mother, LBM, was a worker in the Workshop of Matching. ZH also had a brother, ZB, who worked in the Workshop of Machining. The social relations of C's family in the factory is shown in Fig. A2.

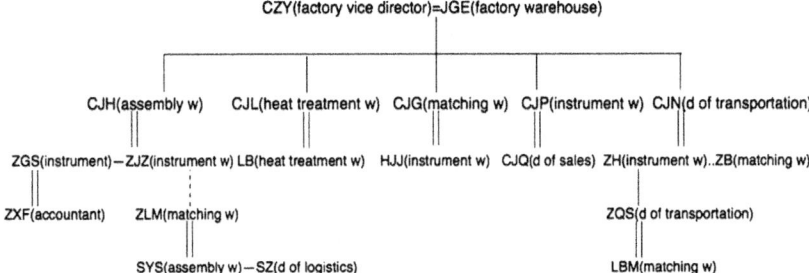

Fig. A2 C's social relations in the factory. (Notes: In this figure, "=" denotes marriage relationship; "..." denotes the relationship of siblings; "_" linking different names indicates people across generations, but not necessarily the parent–child relations. "W" denotes "workshop", while "d" denotes "department")

Index[1]

---

[1] Note: Page numbers followed by 'n' refer to notes.

© The Author(s) 2018

C. Chen, *Toleration*, New Perspectives on Chinese Politics and Society, https://doi.org/10.1007/978-981-10-8941-1

Printed by Printforce, the Netherlands